Physical Characteristics of the English Springer Spaniel

(from The Kennel Club breed standard)

P9-CBC-723

HINDQUARTERS
Hindlegs well let down. Stifles and hocks moderately bent. Thighs broad, muscular, well developed. Coarse hocks undesirable.

TAIL
Set low, never carried above level of back. Well feathered with lively action. Customarily docked.

COAT
Close, straight and weather resisting, never coarse. Moderate feathering on ears, forelegs, body and hindquarters.

COLOUR
Liver and white, black and white, or either of these colours with tan markings.

FEET
Tight, compact, well rounded, with strong, full pads.

SIZE
Approximate height 51 cms (20 ins.).

English Springer Spaniel

◆

by Haja van Wessem

Table of Contents

9

33

28

38

62

DISTRUIBUTED BY:

INTERPET
PUBLISHING

Vincent Lane, Dorking
Surrey RH4 3YX
England

ISBN 978-1-902389-26-4

82

PHOTO CREDITS

Photos by Carol Ann Johnson and Haja van Wessem, with additional photos by:

Norvia Behling
Carolina Biological Supply
Karin Brostam
Doskocil
Isabelle Francais
James Hayden-Yoav
James R Hayden, RBP
Bill Jonas
Dwight R Kuhn

Dr Dennis Kunkel
Mikki Pet Products
Phototake
A H de Raad
Jean Claude Revy
Dr Andrew Spielman
Karen Taylor
C James Webb

Illustrations by Renée Low
Special thanks to Evelyn & Tyce W Beede and Sylvie Linossier, and all owners of dogs featured in this book.

109

Housebreaking and Training Your English Springer Spaniel

by Charlotte Schwartz

Be informed about the importance of training your English Springer Spaniel from the basics of housebreaking, and understanding the development of a young dog, to executing obedience commands (sit, stay, down, etc.).

138

Health Care of Your English Springer Spaniel

Discover how to select a proper veterinary surgeon and care for your dog at all stages of life. Topics include vaccination scheduling, skin problems, dealing with external and internal parasites and the specific congenital health problems of the breed.

Your Senior English Springer Spaniel

Recognise the signs of an aging dog, both behavioural and medical; implement a senior-care programme with your veterinary surgeon and become comfortable with making the final decisions and arrangements for your senior English Springer Spaniel.

145

Showing Your English Springer Spaniel

Experience the dog show world, including different types of shows and the making up of a champion. Go beyond the conformation ring to field trials, working trials and agility trials, etc.

All rights reserved.
No part of this book may be reproduced in any form, by photostat, scanner, microfilm, xerography or any other means, or incorporated into any information retrieval system, electronic or mechanical, without the written permission of the copyright owner.

Copyright © 1999, **2005** • Kennel Club Books®
Cover design patented: US 6,435,559 B2
Printed in South Korea

History of the
ENGLISH SPRINGER SPANIEL

EARLY SPANIEL HISTORY

Spaniels can be considered amongst the oldest dogs in history. Their origins go back a very long time. It is very likely that the spaniel got his name from the countries surrounding the Mediterranean where he lived, 'namely' Spain. He might also have gotten his name from the Basque word *Espana* or from the several spaniel-like breeds in France that are called *épagneuls*. The name spaniel might also be derived from the French *s'espagner*, which means to crouch.

Proof of the antiquity of the breed can be seen in the first mention of a spaniel in Irish Laws in A.D. 17 in a statement that water spaniels had been given as a tribute to the King. Spaniels also travelled to Wales where they were the treasured dogs of King Howell Dha (Howell the Good). The King's love for his spaniels went as far as giving them a special mention in one of the country's laws in A.D. 94: for the price of one spaniel, one could buy a number of goats, women, slaves or geese!

From its ancient beginnings, the English Springer Spaniel has evolved into one of the most well-rounded dog breeds—working dog, champion in all areas of the dog sport and, of course, a favourite amongst pet owners.

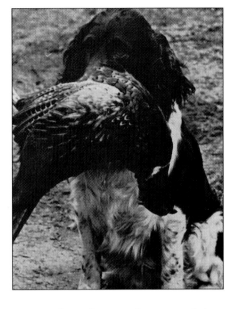

A working Springer Spaniel from Holland, where the breed is very popular.

In these laws a division of the mammals was made into birds, beasts and dogs. The dogs were subdivided into trackers, greyhounds and spaniels.

The first mention of a spaniel in English literature comes as early as Geoffrey Chaucer (1340–1400) and Gaston de Foix, who died in 1391. Chaucer, the poet of *Canterbury Tales*, refers to the spaniel several times (e.g., 'for as a Spaynel she wol on him lepe'), which proves that the spaniel was known in England 600 years ago. Gaston de Foix mentions the spaniel in his work

Miroir de Phoebus or, as it is also known, *Livre de Chasse*. Gaston de Foix, a feudal baron who lived in France near the Spanish border, was convinced that Spain was the country of origin of the spaniel. 'Another manner of hound there is, called hounds for the hawk, and Spaniels, for their kind came from Spain, notwithstanding that there be many in other countries. Such hounds have many good customs and evil. Also a fair hound for the hawk should have a great head, a great body, and be of fair hue, white or tawny (i.e., pied, speckled, or mottled), for they be fairest and of such hue they be commonly the best.' He then describes them as being 'hounds (the word dog was then not used) with a great head and a great, strong body. Their colour is red and white of orange roan, but black and white can also be seen. They run and wag their tail and raise or start fowl and wild beasts. Their right craft is the partridge and the quail. They can also be taught to take partridge and quail with the net and they love to swim.'

A group of handsome working Springer Spaniels from the Netherlands.

Another early reference to *spanyellys* occurs in the *Boke of St. Albans* (1486), also named *The Book of Field Sports*, written by Dame Juliana Berners, prioress of Sopwell Nunnery, Hertfordshire. It is obviously a school book and it is assumed that the book was written for the use of King Henry IV's son, Prince Henry, to teach him to read and make him acquainted with the names of the animals and phrases used in venery and field sports. In the book there is frequent mention of spaniels in the royal household. Thus we read that 'Robin, the King's Majesty's Spaniel Keeper' was paid a certain sum for 'hair cloth to rub the Spaniels with.'

THE FIRST SPRINGERS

We find the first mention of springer spaniels in the book *Treatise of Englishe Dogges* (1570) by the famed dog scholar Dr Caius (pseudonym for John Keyes). Dr Caius described the way the dogs were taught to let themselves be caught under the net and classified all sporting dogs under two headings: *Venatici*, used for the purpose of hunting beasts, and *Auscupatorii*, used for the hunting of fowl. He subdivided this latter group into land spaniels and 'Spaniells which findeth game on the water.' He named this group *Hispaniolus*. He also was of the opinion that these dogs originated

11

in Spain. He describes them as white with red markings or the rarer solid red or black. The land spaniels were praised for their work of springing game for the hounds and the hawks to chase.

In the days of Henry VIII the many royal banquets required a lot of food, and game was an important part. Game such as partridges, quail and pheasant, rabbits and hares were caught in snares but because of the never-ending demand, a more speedy method of catching the game was needed. This method was found in 'netting.' Spaniels were used to drive the birds towards the

fowlers who stood ready with their extended nets. Dog and bird were caught under the net. The spaniels that were used for this kind of work were called sitting or setting spaniels, and they are the ancestors of our modern setters.

With the invention of the gun, netting disappeared and game was caught by shooting. The setting spaniels were used to find the game and point it, and the springing spaniel flushed the game from the cover so that it could be shot.

In the *Sportsman's Cabinet*, written by Nicolas Cox and published in 1803, we find this description of the spaniel: 'The race of dogs passing under the denomination of spaniels are of two kinds, one of which is considerably larger than the other, and are known by the appellation of the springing spaniel—as applica-

No gundog can be a champion without proving his working ability. Illustrated here is the English Springer Spaniel Club at a 1925 field trial at Wootton, near Bedford.

ble to every kind of game in every country: the smaller is called the cocker or cocking spaniel, as being more adapted to covert and woodcock shooting, to which they are more particularly appropriated and by nature seem designed.' We may assume, therefore, that the Cocker Spaniel derives his name from the woodcock or—as some believe—the cockpheasant.

In the 16th and 17th century, another group of spaniels was recognised: the toy spaniels. Since the toy spaniel in those days was bigger and heavier in build than our modern toy spaniels, it is very likely that there was a relationship amongst the Blenheim Spaniel, the King Charles Spaniel and the hunting spaniels. Moreover, it wasn't unusual for Blenheim Spaniels to be used in the field.

In the 18th century, the term springing spaniel was gaining ground as a description, not of a particular variety but of the group

Rufton Repeater, owned by JA Wenger, was considered an excellent specimen of the breed in the 1920s.

of gundogs that sprung their game. All land spaniels came under this heading and the varieties we now know as Clumber, Welsh and English Springer, Field, Cocker and Sussex Spaniel were all springing spaniels.

In the beginning of 1800, the Boughey family of Aqualate in Shropshire developed a distinct strain of spaniel that they bred very carefully and for which they kept a studbook for over a century. After 100 years of selective breeding, an English Springer

A working English Springer Spaniel swiftly and eagerly runs to his master to deliver the booty (in this case, a rabbit).

English Springer Spaniel

It is likely that the King Charles Spaniel, considered one of the toy spaniels, is related to the hunting spaniels.

The English Cocker Spaniel was classified as a cocking spaniel.

Spaniel was born in 1903 that was to become famous as Field Trial Champion Velox Powder, owned by C Eversfield of 'Denne' Springers. Velox Powder traces back to Mop I, the first dog to appear in the Aqualate register in 1812. The Boughey family kept their interest in English Springers until the 1930s.

In the late 1800s, there was a great interest for Springer Spaniels because of their outstanding working abilities. The Sandringham Kennels of King Edward VII in Norfolk contained many fine Springers that were known for some time as Norfolk Spaniels. Not only in Norfolk but also in other parts of England, all parti-coloured spaniels were known as Norfolk Spaniels until after 1900 when they all became Springer Spaniels.

In those early days Springer Spaniel breeders used other breeds to fix the English Springer Spaniel type. In the very early 1900s, Mr Phillips bred a Cocker Spaniel bitch to an English Springer to produce the winning Springer Ch Rivington Sam.

Breeders have also made use of English Setters, Pointers and even a Clumber to improve the bone on the dogs. The story goes that Field Spaniels have been used to improve the English Springer's heads. Orange-coloured puppies from a litter with an English Setter were registered as Welsh Springers. A daughter of the famous Beechgrove Will was registered as a Field Spaniel.

In 1885 the Spaniel Club was founded. The first field trial was held in 1899 on Mr William Arkwright's estate in Derbyshire. Mr James Farrow and Mr C A Phillips were the judges. However, it was not English Springer Spaniel but a Clumber Spaniel, Beechgrove Bee, owned by Mr F Winton Smith, who won. A year later it was an English Springer Spaniel by the name of Tring who took the top honours.

In 1902, The Kennel Club recognised the English Springer Spaniel as a specific variety of spaniel and the Spaniel Club drew up the standard for the breed and submitted it to The Kennel Club for approval. It was not long before the first Springers became bench champions. Beechgrove Will of Mr Winton Smith was the first dog to become a champion and Major Harry Jones's Fansom was the first bitch to do so. The first English Springer to become Field Trial Champion, in 1913, was Rivington Sam, out of the Cocker bitch Rivington Ribbon

The Clumber Spaniel was used in early breeding programmes to improve the Springer's bone.

and by Spot of Hagley. Sam was the grandsire of Field Trial Champion Rex of Avendale, who features in the pedigrees of many of our modern English Springers.

In 1921, the English Springer Spaniel Club was founded and the breed enjoyed increasing popularity. The early pioneers held strongly to the view that the English Springer was basically a working dog and their aim was to breed for working abilities as well as breed conformation.

Many famous breeders and

affixes from those early days can be remembered, such as Mr Winton Smith (Beechgrove); Mr H S Lloyd (Of Ware); the Duke of Hamilton (Avendale); Mr C A Phillips (Rivington); Mr C C Eversfield (Denne) and Lady Portal (Laverstoke).

The Welsh Springer Spaniel is a close relative of the English Springer.

HISTORY OF THE BREED IN GREAT BRITAIN

Until 1920 the fanciers of the breed were not much interested in showing. They worked their Springers and the only breeders

The Sussex Spaniel is another of the springing spaniels.

A beautiful head study of Foxfield Alpha, owned by R Bowden. This dog was a huge winner, including Challenge Certificates, in 1932 and 1933.

Regalia, owned by Miss Morland Hooper, retrieves a moorhen. The dog holds the bird very lightly and is very serious about its work.

who used to show their Springers were Mr W Arkwright and Mr F Winton Smith.

Still, the breed did well because the Springer was not only a much loved pet but was also very helpful in bringing in rabbit, which was a very important food for many country families between the two wars.

Notable stud dogs in the first two decades of the century were: Ch Velox Powder, Ch Rivington Sam, Ch Rex of Avendale, Ch Flint of Avendale, Ch Springbok of Ware and Ch. Denne Duke. Mr C A Phillips's Rivington dogs were a strong force for a consider-

able period of time. As late as 1951, Rivington Glensaugh Glean won the Spaniel Championships. His name appears in many pedigrees and he has sired at least eight field trial champions.

Notable breeders in the years between the two wars were: Hon George Scott (Marmion), Mr R Grierson (of Solway), Miss Morland Hooper (Ranscombe) and Mr H S Lloyd (the internationally famous 'Wizard of Ware') who was world famous not only for his Cockers but also for his Springers. Ch Springbok, Ch Jambok and Ch Jamson of Ware were well-known winners and sires. Ch Springbok of Ware eventually went to the States.

As with so many breeds and clubs, World War II put an end to all activities. Shows and breeding were restarted after the war, but it took some time before the breeders had attained the pre-war level of quality.

Although not often shown, Boxer of Bramhope, owned by

Mrs Mary Scott, had a tremendous influence on the breed as a sire; and he features in almost every pedigree. The Bramhope Kennels produced a great number of winners and famous sons of Boxer are Ch Alexander of Stubham, Ch Peter of Lortonfell and Ch Studley Major.

New breeders after the war were Joe Braddon (of Ide) and Andrew and Jimmy Wylie (Pinehawk). The Wylie brothers produced many field trial winners.

In the 1950s, The Kennel Club decided to change the rules for winning the title of champion. Until then a dog could only become a champion if he had won three Challenge Certificates (CCs) and a qualifier in the field. In the

Ch Banchory Boy, belonging to the Countess of Howe, offering a retrieved rabbit. Circa 1934.

'50s The Kennel Club decided to introduce the title of Show Champion for a dog that had won three CCs and Champion for the dog that had won three CCs and had also qualified in the field. A Dual Champion is a dog that has obtained the title of Show Champion and Field Trial Champion as well. The number of Springers that have become Dual Champions is small. Amongst them are Horsford Hetman and his son Thoughtful of Harting as well as Flint of Avendale, who later went to Canada.

The first dogs to win the new title of Show Champion were Bonaventura of Bramhope, Stokeley Sea Sprite and Sandylands Susanna. Mrs Hanna Stokeley was

'Lonely?' That was the caption for Sidbrook Ranger, owned by Mr Hebstrip. This photo was taken by Keystone at the 1937 Crufts Dog Show.

A Spaniel painting by Reinagle, circa 1830, shows a Springer Spaniel after having flushed the ducks.

order to do so they had to win four CCs at shows as well as qualify in the field.

Alexander of Stubham, owned by Mrs F Oughtred Till, won 22 CCs, which was a record for those days, and he joined his sire Boxer of Bramhope as one of the leading stud dogs in the breed.

In the '60s and '70s, competition was very strong and very few new faces were seen in the ring.

Am Ch Salilyn's Condor was Top Dog All Breeds in 1992 and Best in Show at Westminster in 1993. Pictured is the Best in Show win.

especially in favour of mixing show and working lines. In 1958, Ch Stokeley Higham Tona was the dam of two field trial winners, Rogue and Scamp, who later went to Italy to Mr Marco Valcarenghi and became Italian champions. In

Am Ch Salilyn's Aristocrat's son, Am Ch Adamant James, took Best in Show at the Westminster show, held in New York, in both 1971 and 1972.

One of the kennels that dominated the ring was Hawkhill, owned by Judith Hancock. In partnership with Jimmy Cudworth, Judith steered Hawkhill Connaught to a position no English Springer had attained before. He was a shared top dog in 1972 and top dog in 1973. He won over 50 CCs and some 16 Groups. St. Pauli Girl of Moorcliff and Prince Consort of Moorcliff were bred by Hawkhill and owned by Ernest Froggat, who bred winners himself including Sh Ch Moorcliff Dougal and Sh Ch Moorcliff Gamecock, who was the sire of the famous Connaught.

On the working side, a famous dog is undoubtedly Hales Smut, owned by Arthur Cooke and bred by Mr Keith Erlandson. He sired at least 13 field trial champions. Mr Erlandson's prefix Gwibernant is well known all over Europe.

Other breeders who certainly

A 1928 painting by Reinagle of what appears to be an ancestor of the Springer Spaniel.

deserve a mention are Mrs O Hampton (Larkstoke), Mrs E Dobson (Tyneview), Mr and Mrs D Miller (Feorlig), Mrs J Taylor (Cleavehill), Mr C Muirhead (Shipden) and Mr and Mrs Woodward (Wadeson)

The dog that caused a (pleasant) stir was certainly Sh Ch Elimvek Earthbound, who was still a youngster when he won the Gundog Group at the Crufts Dog Show in 1998. He was the top winning English Springer Spaniel of 1998, closely followed by Sh Ch Wadeson Inspector Wexford,

another Group and Best in Show winner.

Although the aim of the club has always been to support field and show, it was unavoidable that a distinct working-type English Springer Spaniel came into being. There is a tendency in working lines to breed for a smaller and lighter dog whereas the show Springer is heavier in bone and larger.

Unfortunately, both the show and working enthusiasts have adopted breeding plans to suit their goals best, be it showing or

Multi-Ch Strathnaver Barley Wine, owned by S Lovenkjaer, was bred in England and imported to Denmark. He became a top-winning dog and a very influential sire in Scandinavia in the 1990s.

Ch Dry Toast was a huge winner in the U.K. during the early 1930s.

Sh Ch Hawkshill Connaught was Top Dog in 1972 and 1973, and the winner of 50 CCs.

Int Ch Springbok of Ware went to the United States, where he also became a champion.

The legendary Am Ch Salilyn's Aristocrat was the top sire of all time, all breeds, as well as the winner of 45 Bests in Show and Top Dog of 1967.

working, and the difference in type has become such that they have almost made the English Springer into two separate breeds.

THE SPRINGER ON THE CONTINENT

The first spaniel to be registered in the Dutch stud book (number. 123) was Wallace, born in January 1889, chestnut brown and white,

very likely a British import and considering his colour, an English Springer.

A while passed before the next registration, but in 1902 one can find the registration of a litter of Cocker Spaniels of whom several later were shown as Springers. Their sire was Rivington Red Coat and their dam Colwyn Rose. Colwyn was the prefix of Mr Porter in England and sever-

al Colwyns have Breasides in their pedigree, both being the prefixes of breeders of Cockers and Springers. We may therefore safely assume that interbreeding between Cockers and Springers took place and that depending on their size the offspring was registered as Cockers, Fields or Springers and maybe even, depending on their colour, as Welsh Springer Spaniels.

In 1925, when the English Springer was surviving but not really thriving, an English Springer by the name of Hick was born. His dam was Shalassa

(Ranger of Ranscombe x Grass Bessie) and his sire Cassio Trooper (Ch Flint of Avendale x Cassion Nixie). Hick was a tri-coloured dog, bred by Mrs A Pike and owned by Mrs L van Herwaarden, who together with her husband had started in Cocker Spaniels (Wagtail). Hick won many championship awards in Holland, Germany and Belgium and proved himself in the field as well.

After the war in 1947, a dog and a bitch were imported: Horsford Hence and Horsford Tara. Their owner, Mr J G Sillem, took the suffix van het Watervliet and bred his first litter with these two in 1948. He bred them again in 1951.

An important import was Winch Crocidolite (Rollicker of Ranscombe x Winch Brown Jewel) born in 1953 and bred by Mrs G G Crawford, owned in Holland by Mr T Plate. In 1956 Winch Crocidolite sired a litter for Mr Cremer

F Warner Hill's Ch Beauchief Benefactor was an outstanding champion of the 1930s.

out of the bitch Wilby Stokedoyle Tina. This was the start of the Van Duin en Kruidberg Kennels that was so successful in later years. Mr Cremer, later in partnership with Mr and Mrs Kingma, built a line of work and show Springers and many champions had the Duin en Kruidberg suffix.

In 1965 Mr G Radsma bred his first Van de Springershoek litter. In this litter a puppy was born that was to become very famous as a show dog and sire: Mizar van de Springershoek. He became a champion in 1968, the second Springer to do so. His litter sister

The top-winning stud dog of 1985 was Sh Ch Chaigmarsh Sudden Impact. His sire, Ardencote Alexander, was also a top-winning stud dog, as well as his offspring, Mompesson Dream Chaser.

Dutch Ch Hick was the dominating Springer in Holland in the 1920s.

English Springers at a championship show in Holland, judged by Mr Mark Hamer of the UK. (Left) Best Bitch, Dutch Ch Snuggle-wood's Zamara. (Right) Best Dog and Best of Breed, Eastriding High-lander.

English Springers at a championship show in Holland, judged by Mr Mark Hamer of the UK. (Left) Best Bitch, Dutch Ch Snugglewood's Zamara. (Right) Best Dog and Best of Breed, Eastriding Highlander.

Sagitta van de Springershoek followed suit a year later.

In 1970 Mr and Mrs Viergever, who as the owners of Ch Mizar

Mompesson Remember Me is the breed record holder in Great Britain with 54 CCs, as well as a qualifier in the field. He is bred and owned by Mrs F Jackson.

van de Springershoek were well into Springers by now, imported a bitch from Britain by the name of Larkstoke Sarcelle, bred by Mrs O Hampton, out of Ch Larkstoke Ptarmigan and by Ch Teesview Tarmac. She had the beauty of her parents and she passed on their working ability to her offspring. Sarcelle was the first English Springer to win a Best in Show in Holland at an international all-breed Championship Show.

By this time the difference in type between working and show Springers became apparent in Holland as in Britain, and the working Springers gained more and more in popularity. The gap between the two types has continued to widen to such an extent that nowadays we seem to have reached a point of no return.

In addition to Mr Cremer and his Van Duen en Kruidberg Kennel, another important breeder of the show Springers was the Dongemond Kennel founded by Mr and Mrs Arendse, which produced many show champions. In the early '80s Mr de Vette imported Saxdalens Dette de Vette from Denmark, and she produced several champions who, in their turn, became the start for other kennels, such as Mr F Derwort's Pool of Buzzard and Mrs M Dingley's Laburnum. Mrs H v d Brink's Van het Veense Springertje started with a Duin en Kruidberg bitch, which was mated to Norfolk's Moby Dick and is now well on its way. Snugglewood is the prefix of Mr C Warmenhoven, best known for its Cockers but they had a

A working Springer of the 1990s in the Netherlands.

good run with their English Springers as well. Dutch Ch Stowequest Trident Lad was an import who did very well in Holland, winning several Groups at international all-breed Championship Shows.

Nowadays the influence of Danish and Swedish breeding becomes more noted, two countries where the show Springers are of a very high standard.

In the field trial lines, we see many more breeders of whom the most successful ones have been: Mr G Visscher's van het Eendebos, Mr R van Stuyvenberg's Dashhill, Mr B Boers' Hauk and Mr J Wintermans v d Steevoerde. A famous import has been Mr van Stuyvenberg's Bonny of Gilcraig, who not only became a Dutch and international field trial champion herself but was the dam of four field trial champions from two litters sired by Kentoo Donald.

The top English Springer Spaniel in Holland in 1996, 1997 and 1998 was Dutch Ch Stowequest Trident Lad, bred in England and owned by C A F Warmenhoven in Holland.

23

Sh Ch Slayleigh Paulina, who was the dam of six Show Champions in Great Britain.

One interesting phenomenon is the import of several 'American-type' English Springers. In the early '90s, the first dogs arrived in Holland of whom Dutch Ch Skywatch's Silverhill Elias became the best known. He was the second Springer to win a Best in Show at an all-breed show.

Although the American bloodlines are well represented in Germany (mainly through Scandinavian imports) and have been used by Scandinavian breeders, the American type never has become very popular in Holland where the English type of Springer still dominates.

Even as an older dog, Am Ch Salilyn's Aristocrat was an elegant, prize-winning sire in the 1960s.

In Holland and Germany, a dog that wins four CCs at Championship Shows becomes a champion. In Denmark, three CCs are sufficient. A dog becomes an international champion when he obtains a qualification in an international field trial as well. In France, he has to obtain a qualification in the field as well as three CCs at shows to become a champion. A field trial champion is a dog that won two championships at an official field trial or one championship and two reserve championships and who, moreover, has obtained the qualification 'Very Good' or 'Excellent' at a show.

THE ENGLISH SPRINGER IN AMERICA

It is interesting to note that the author of a book written in the early 1600s (*Journal of the English Plantation at Plymouth* by G Mourt) reported that there were two dogs on board the Mayflower, a mastiff and a spaniel.

The Springer Spaniel has long been very popular in the United States. They were used to work in swamplands and brambles, just as in England. Later, because of the growing popularity of setters and pointers, their number declined to such an extent that the breed was threatened with extinction, but thanks to the Sporting Spaniel Society and the breeders it was saved. They set out to re-develop the Springer Spaniel by using the liver-and-white and black-and-

Scandinavia's top-winning Springer is Multi-Ch Whisborne Devil in Disguise, bred in Sweden and owned by Jesse Madsen of Sieger English Springers in Denmark.

Worthing Surprise, exhibited in 1934, shows a lovely head with a clearly defined stop. Owned by Mrs T Ford-Lowe.

New York, followed by the first field trial in 1924. Best of Breed at the show was Horsford Highness, a son of Horsford Hetman.

In 1924 the American Kennel Club recognised the standard for the English Springer Spaniel after the foundation of the English Springer Spaniel Trial Association. In 1932 this standard was replaced by another.

Mr Chevrier was a breed enthusiast who lived in Canada and it is for a great part thanks to him that the breed is so well

white Keepers Spaniels, the Clumber, the old English Water Spaniel, the Sussex, the setter and spaniel-crosses that were owned by sportsmen. They succeeded and, as the breed revived, interest increased and many imports from the UK contributed to a wider genetic base for the breed.

The first official registration was in 1910 and the first show with classes for Springers was in 1923 in Madison Square Garden,

Compare this typical working Springer with the show dogs. This is Field Trial Ch Silverstar of Chrishall.

25

An English dog being exhibited at an outdoor show.

established in the United States and Canada. In three-and-a-half years' time, up to 1925, he imported 250 dogs from England, including Field Trial Champion Flint of Avendale, Field Trial Champion Dan of Avendale, Ch Springbok of Ware and many others. In 1925 there were 600 Springers in his kennels and at the Westminster Show he showed 11 Springers!

In the '50s and '60s a lot of good-quality English Springers found their way from Great Britain to the States, and since then the breed has prospered. The most famous breeder in the United States is undoubtedly Mrs Julia Gasow of the Salilyn prefix, and the most famous dog is without a doubt Ch Salilyn's Aristocrat, who won 45 Bests in Show, was number-one sire all time, all breeds with 188 champion offspring. He

An English dog being exhibited at an outdoor show.

was top dog in 1967. His grandson Ch Salilyn's Private Stock and his great-grandson Ch Salilyn's Classic each produced more than a hundred champions. His son Ch Chinoe's Adamant James won Best in Show at Westminster in 1971 and 1972. He was top dog in 1971. His great-grandson Ch Salilyn's Condor was top dog all breeds in 1992 and Best in Show at Westminster in 1993.

As in England the gap between the show and working Springers has widened and could not be bridged anymore. Apart from that, the American

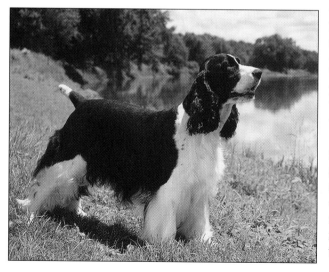

Today's English Springer excels as a working dog, a show dog and a family pet.

Head studies of (left) an American dog and (right) a dog from the UK. The American Springer is the famous Ch Salilyn's Aristocrat.

breeders have nowadays created a show dog that has its own, very distinct type, and the difference between English and American Springer Spaniels has become just as notable as the difference between show and working type.

The American Springers are mostly all 'open marked,' i.e., black and white or liver and white without any ticking, they have more coat and are slightly more cocker-like in type, especially in head. They are slightly smaller (50 cms in the British standard and 46 cms in the American stan-dard). Although different in type, it is without any doubt a beautiful dog and that is one of the reasons why fanciers of both the American and the English type suggested that the American Springer Spaniel be recognised as a separate breed.

27

PERSONALITY OF THE
ENGLISH SPRINGER SPANIEL

Once you have decided that you want to share your life with a dog, the next question is: which breed is it going to be? You must determine which breed suits you best in temperament and in lifestyle, and what do you plan to do with your new puppy? Do you want to work on your condition and that of your dog by joining agility classes? Would you like to do obedience training or are you so fortunate as to be able to take a dog on a shoot?

English Springers are often the hunting dogs of choice because they are skilled workers with gentle mouths as well as pleasant companions. They are intelligent dogs and, thus, easily trained.

If we look at the official description of the English Springer Spaniel, the first words that strike us are 'strong, merry, active.' That is what an English Springer Spaniel is. A Springer Spaniel is a happy, even-natured dog. Like all the other spaniels, he has the innate desire to please, which makes him a good dog to work with as well as a loveable companion. His is a faithful and cheerful personality. He is happy to work and happy to play; he is the ultimate optimist. He gets up every morning in the joyful expectation of another lovely day, with lots of fun, hopefully a lot to eat because he loves his food, and who knows what new and exciting adventures! If you take him on a walk, he will expect to find game behind every blade of grass, and in the show ring he will give his all for you. He loves to share his happiness with everybody, and if this means that he jumps up on you with four muddy paws, you have to understand that in the spirit with which it was done! His happy, easygoing temperament also makes him a fatalist. If he cannot come with you he will express his great sorrow (and he can look very sorrowful!), but he will accept the situation and make the best of it. If his feet are to be trimmed he will try to wriggle out of it, but if you are firm he will give a mental shrug and go to sleep on the trimming table. This behaviour makes it very important that you are gentle but firm with him, because he is clever enough to realise that if he gets his way once, he may get it again, and again.

Although your Springer may think that every guest to your house has been especially invited to please him and will therefore be loved by him, he is very loyal and affectionate to his own people. He not only shares your house he also shares your life, your joys and your sorrows. He has a special antenna for your moods. The bond between you and your Springer can become incredibly strong to the point that no words are needed.

ARE YOU A SPRINGER PERSON?
Other distinctions of the Springer that deserve mention is that he is the oldest of the sporting gundogs and that his original purpose was finding and springing game. Nowadays he is used for finding, flushing and retrieving game and he not only is very good at it he also loves to work for you.

This means that you have to provide an outlet for his active and lively nature. You must be prepared to give your Springer, when he has matured, at least an hour of free exercise every day. Whilst he will enjoy a walk

through the park on the lead, or even a shopping expedition, he needs to have the opportunity to stretch his legs, run at full speed and be able to pick up exciting smells that appeal to his hunting instinct. Woods, fields, dunes, he loves them all, but he especially loves water. If the idea of a soaking wet and rather muddy dog doesn't appeal to you, you have to teach him right from the start to stay away from the water. Don't think that will be easy! In the eyes of a Springer, a walk without a swim is only half a walk but, if necessary, a romp in a deep, preferably muddy puddle will also do!

Springers love the water! Walks and runs are great exercise, but the Springer will always welcome the opportunity to go for a swim.

29

English Springer Spaniel

Although a sporting dog by nature, the Springer makes a wonderful pet and is a popular choice for many families.

The Springer's energy is endless. He will walk the same distance as you do two or three times over, at full speed, without resting—and it only takes the ten-minute drive home in the car to restore him. Once home, he would like you to play with him, throw a ball for him to fetch or other activities to get rid of his energy.

In recent years the working ability of the breed has been extended and performances have improved in speed and style. This may bring the risk of exaggeration and you may end up with a hyperactive dog who is more difficult to train. For the average owner, such a Springer is just a bit too much to cope with.

You have to make up your mind beforehand: will you want to train him for field trials? Then very likely a good Springer from sensible trainable lines will be the best all round gundog for you

Do you want to show? Then find a breeder who breeds lovely and healthy Springers of good quality and you'll have a gentle companion who will love his outings with you and whose will to please makes him the perfect show dog.

Do you just want a pet? Then you can choose either but bear in mind that a Springer as a pet needs all the exercise and training a show or working Springer needs.

If you live in a flat or in the centre of a city, I would not recommend a Springer. They can adapt to any environment, but as a working dog they need open areas where they can have proper exercise and use their normal instincts for hunting and enjoying the scents of the countryside. Town parks and recreation fields are not enough.

Now that you have decided on a Springer Spaniel, there still are a few questions that need to be answered before you can go to a breeder. What colour would you like? Will it be a dog or a bitch? It is often said that a bitch is sweeter than a dog, but in my experience the dogs are just as sweet as the bitches and very easygoing. It is very important that you explain all your preferences to the breeder so that he can help you pick the puppy that is best suited to you.

If you have a family with children, it might be wiser not to buy a dominant puppy because the puppy will have several 'masters' and will end up not listening to anybody. In a slightly dominant dog, that may cause problems! In a litter the personalities of the puppies may differ slightly. Explain to the breeder what you prefer: the softer, sweeter one, or the outgoing, cheeky puppy?

If you have the time and dedication to train your puppy and treat him consistently at all times, there is no better pet than an English Springer Spaniel. By choosing an English Springer Spaniel, you have chosen a companion with a very happy temperament, who thinks life is wonderful and who will love you indiscriminately.

COAT COLOURS

Dr Caius mentioned in his *Treatise of Dogges* (1570), the Aquaticus or Spanyell who finds game in the water and who is either red and white, solid black or solid red. In 1803 in the book *The Sportsman's Cabinet*, springing

spaniels and cocking spaniels are mentioned in the colours black and white, liver and white and red and white.

In 1933 the English Springer Spaniel Club decided that all the colours of the original land spaniels would be permissible with the exception of the typical

red and white which is restricted to the Welsh Springer Spaniels. Thus the official colours for the English Springer Spaniels are black and white, liver and white, black, white and tan and liver, white and tan.

Although either black and white or liver and white (with or without tan markings) are allowed, the popular colour has always been, and still is, liver and white with or without ticking.

Two Springers cuddle up with their Cocker Spaniel friend.

31

Breed Standard for the
ENGLISH SPRINGER SPANIEL

The first breed standard was written and officially approved by the English Kennel Club in 1902. In later years some minor changes have been made, but on the whole the standard has remained practically unaltered; the latest, included here, standard dates from 1986. This standard is also officially recognised in all of the FCI countries. The FCI (Fédération Cynologique Internationale) includes the kennel clubs in the following countries: nearly all continental European countries, Argentina, Brazil, Chile, Colombia, Ecuador, Mexico, Panama, Paraguay, Peru, Puerto Rico, Dominican Republic, Uruguay, Venezuela, and furthermore Israel, Morocco, South Korea, Japan, Philippines, Thailand. There are several other countries which are not affiliated with the FCI but associated, such as Bulgaria, Cyprus, Greece, Rumania, San Marino, Bermuda, Bolivia, Costa Rica, Cuba, Guatemala, Honduras, Ireland, Hong Kong, India, Indonesia, Malaysia, Singapore, Sri Lanka, Taiwan, Madagascar, South Africa, Zimbabwe, Australia and New Zealand. In these countries the British standard is the official breed standard. The breed standard as approved by the American Kennel Club is slightly different, certainly more extensive, and with a slight difference in the ideal size and weight.

This is what a champion English Springer looks like! In order to succeed in the conformation ring, a dog must adhere very closely to its breed standard.

(top) Correct head. (bottom) Incorrect head; too snipey.

Temperament: Friendly, happy disposition, biddable. Timidity or aggression highly undesirable.

Head and Skull: Skull of medium length, fairly broad, slightly rounded, rising from foreface, making a brow or stop, divided by fluting between eyes, dying away along forehead towards occipital bone which should not be prominent. Cheeks flat. Foreface of proportionate length to skull, fairly broad and deep, well chiselled below eyes, fairly deep and square in flew. Nostrils well developed.

THE KENNEL CLUB BREED STANDARD FOR THE ENGLISH SPRINGER SPANIEL
General Appearance: Symmetrically built, compact, strong, merry, active. Highest on leg and raciest in build of all British land Spaniels.

Characteristics: Breed is of ancient and pure origins, oldest of sporting gundogs; original purpose was finding and springing game for net, falcon or greyhound. Now used to find, flush and retrieve game for gun.

(top) Correct eye. (bottom) Incorrect eye with haw showing.

Eyes: Medium size, almond shaped, not prominent nor sunken, well set in (not showing haw), alert, kind expression. Dark hazel. Light eyes undesirable.

Ears: Lobular, good length and width, fairly close to head, set in line with eye. Nicely feathered.

Mouth: Jaws strong, with a perfect, regular and complete scissor bite, i.e., upper teeth closely overlapping lower teeth and set square to the jaws.

Neck: Good length, strong and muscular, free from throatiness, slightly arched, tapering towards head.

Forequarters: Forelegs straight and well boned. Elbows set well to body. Strong flexible pasterns.

Body: Strong, neither too long nor too short. Chest deep, well developed. Well sprung ribs. Loin muscular, strong with slight arch and well coupled.

Hindquarters: Hindlegs well let down. Stifles and hocks moderately bent. Thighs broad, muscular, well developed. Coarse hocks undesirable.

Feet: Tight, compact, well rounded, with strong full pads.

(top) Correct head with flat cheeks.
(bottom) Incorrect; rounded cheeks.

(left) Correct muscular hindquarters.
(right) Incorrect hindquarters.

(left) Correct straight forelegs.
(right) Incorrect forelegs; elbows turning out.

(left) Correct length and back. Loin slightly arched. (right) Incorrect; back too long and loin flat.

Tail: Set low, never carried above level of back. Well feathered with lively action. Customarily docked.

Gait/Movement: Strictly his own. Forelegs swing straight forward from shoulder, throwing feet well forward in an easy free manner. Hocks driving well under body, following in line with forelegs. At slow movement may have a pacing stride typical of this breed.

Coat: Close, straight and weather resisting, never coarse. Moderate feathering on ears, forelegs, body and hindquarters.

Colour: Liver and white, black and white, or either of these colours with tan markings.

Size: Approximate height: 51 cms (20 ins).

Faults: Any departure from the foregoing points should be considered a fault and the seriousness with which the fault should be regarded should be in exact proportion to its degree.

Note: Male animals should have two apparently normal testicles fully descended into the scrotum.

A champion-quality English Springer Spaniel being exhibited in the UK.

FINDING A BREEDER

Once you have decided that it is an English Springer with whom you want to share your life, your next step is to find a breeder. It may help you to visit a couple of dog shows or a breed club Championship Show. Watch the breeders and how they communicate with their dogs, look at the dogs and see which breeder has dogs with the type and temperament that you like. You can also contact the breed club and ask for names and addresses of breeders with puppies for sale. The club will give you a list of breeders who have puppies that fulfil the club rules. These rules mainly concern matters of hereditary defects in both parents.

If the breeders whose dogs you like are not on the list, do not hesitate to contact them and ask if they will have puppies in the future and whether these puppies will fulfil the club rules. If you visit a breeder and you are a bit doubtful about the puppies or the breeder or the conditions in which the puppies are kept, or if the breeder thinks that checking for hereditary defects is not necessary, don't buy! It must be a 100% decision. Buying a pup because you are afraid to say no or because you feel sorry for the pup is wrong. After all, you are going to buy a companion for the next 12–14 years and you must be absolutely sure that he is the one you want and no other!

Although the English Springer Spaniel is a healthy breed, there are a few breed-related hereditary conditions. Responsible breeders will have their stock examined for these conditions and will not breed from affected stock. Defects that can sometimes occur are:

Hip dysplasia is a degeneration of the hip socket into which the femoral head rests. It is common in most breeds of purebred dogs.

Did You Know?

Your selection of a good puppy can be determined by your needs. A show potential, a field dog or a good pet? It is your choice. Every puppy, however, should be of good temperament. Although show-quality puppies are bred and raised with emphasis on physical conformation, responsible breeders strive for equally good temperament. Whether field, show or pet, all Springers must have stable temperaments and sound health.

Are You a Fit Owner?

If the breeder from whom you are buying a puppy asks you a lot of personal questions, do not be insulted. Such a breeder wants to be sure that you will be a fit provider for his puppy.

Children and puppies naturally make the best of friends! When choosing a puppy, all members of the family should participate in the decision.

Progressive retinal atrophy is a congenital disease of the eye that affects the Springer as well as many other purebred dogs.

Cataracts, a condition whereby the lens will become covered with a milky film, is often seen in older dogs (ten years and older). Since ageing is a gradual process, it is not much cause for urgent concern when a cataract begins to form. However, there is another form of cataract that occurs at an early age, affecting the eyesight of the dog and therefore is much more serious.

Retinal dysplasia, another eye condition, in its mildest form is seen as a multiple folding of the retina that has no influence on the eyesight, and in its most serious form is a non-attachment of the retina to the underlying choroid and can lead to blindness.

Should you want to buy a puppy for showing, discuss with the breeder what to do in case the puppy will not be showable. Its mouth may go wrong, if it's a male he may turn out to be

monorchid (only one descended testicle), etc. If you are very determined to have a show-quality pup, you might do better to buy a more mature puppy, say six to

Did You Know?

Breeders rarely release puppies until they are eight to ten weeks of age. This is an acceptable age for most breeds of dog, excepting toy breeds which are not released until around 12 weeks, given their petite sizes. If a breeder has a puppy that is 12 weeks or more, it is likely well socialised and housetrained. Be sure that it is otherwise healthy before deciding to take it home.

39

seven months, so that these risks cannot occur. Enquire about inoculations and when the puppy was last dosed for worms.

Nowadays puppies are often sold with a sales contract. This is fine, but don't sign on the spot. Ask the breeder if you can take it home to read it carefully so that you know exactly what you are signing. More important than a sales contract, however, is a good relationship between you and the breeder. A responsible, dedicated breeder is at all times willing to answer all your questions, to calm your fears and to share your joys.

SELECTING A PUPPY

You contacted a breeder, he has a litter and there you are, surrounded by all these lovely puppies. How will you ever be able to choose! You have decided that you want a

Did You Know?

Your puppy should have a well-fed appearance but not a distended abdomen, which may indicate worms or incorrect feeding, or both. The body should be firm, with a solid feel. The skin of the abdomen should be pale pink and clean, without signs of scratching or rash. Check the hind legs to make certain that dewclaws were removed, if any were present at birth.

bitch puppy so ask the breeder to take the dog puppies away, that makes it a bit easier. Now what you are looking for is a healthy, good-looking, happy little thing that will be all over you when you crouch down, thinking you are great fun. Don't go for shy puppies but don't go for the bullies either! Ask the breeder if you can see the dam (and sire, if possible) and see what her temperament is like. Discuss the pedigree with him, so that you can make sure that your puppy comes from good stock.

A ten-week-old Springer puppy should have a fairly long head with a well-defined stop, a good reach of neck, good ribs and good quarters with hocks well let down. Shoulders should be laid back, front legs straight. The set of the tail should be a little below the level of the back and should be carried straight with lively action.

The puppy should have nice tight dark eyes. Take care to look for damp patches around the eyes because that means that there is something amiss. A good shiny coat is an indication of good health as is a happy and exuberant temperament.

Remember, you cannot be too careful when it comes to deciding on the type of dog you want and finding out about your prospective pup's background. Buying a puppy is not—or should not be—just another whimsical purchase. In fact, this is one instance in which

The decision can be difficult when choosing an adorable Springer puppy.

you actually do get to choose your own family! But, you may be thinking, buying a puppy should be fun—it should not be so serious and so much work. Keep in mind that your puppy is not a cuddly stuffed toy or decorative lawn ornament, but instead will become a real member of your family. Thus, you will realise that, whilst buying a puppy is a pleasurable and exciting endeavour, it is not something to be taken lightly. Relax...the fun will start when the pup comes home!

Your Schedule ...

If you lead an erratic, unpredictable life, with daily or weekly changes in your work requirements, consider the problems of owning a puppy. The new puppy has to be fed regularly, socialised (loved, petted, handled, introduced to other people) and, most importantly, allowed to visit outdoors for toilet training. As the dog gets older, it can be more tolerant of deviations in its feeding and toilet relief.

Bear in mind that a puppy is nothing more than a baby in a furry disguise...a baby who is virtually helpless in a human world and who trusts his owner for fulfilment of his basic needs for survival. That goes beyond food, water and shelter; your pup needs care, protection, guidance and love. If you are not prepared to commit to this, then you are not prepared to own a dog.

Do not worry too much as you will probably find that once your pup gets used to his new home, he will fall into his place in the family quite naturally. But it never hurts to emphasise the commitment of dog ownership. With some time and patience, it is really not too difficult to raise a curious and exuberant Springer Spaniel pup to be a well-adjusted and well-mannered adult dog—a dog that could be your most loyal friend.

♀ Boy or Girl? ♂

An important consideration to be discussed is the sex of your puppy. For a family companion, a bitch may be the better choice, considering the female's inbred concern for all young creatures and her accompanying tolerance and patience. It is always advised to spay a pet bitch, which may guarantee her a longer life.

PREPARING PUPPY'S PLACE IN YOUR HOME

Researching your breed and finding a breeder are only two aspects of the 'homework' you will have to do before bringing your puppy home. You will also have to prepare your home and family for the new addition. Much like you would prepare a nursery for a newborn baby, you will need to designate a place in your home that will be the puppy's own. How you prepare your home will depend on how much freedom the dog will be allowed. Whatever you decide, you must ensure that he has a place that he can 'call his own.'

When you bring your new puppy into your home, you are bringing him into what will become his home as well. Obviously, you did not buy a puppy so that he could take over your house, but in order for a puppy to grow into a stable, well-adjusted dog, he has to feel comfortable in his surroundings. Remember, he is leaving the warmth and security of his mother and littermates, as well as the familiarity of the only place he has ever known, so it is important to make his transition as easy as possible. By preparing a place in your home for the puppy, you are making him feel as welcome as possible in a strange new place. It should not take him long to get used to it, but the sudden shock of being transplanted is somewhat traumatic for a young pup. Imagine how a small child would feel in the same situation—that is how your puppy must be feeling. It is up to you to reassure him and to let him know, 'Little fellow, you are going to like it here!'

WHAT YOU SHOULD BUY
CRATE
To someone unfamiliar with the use of crates in dog training, it may seem like punishment to shut a dog in a crate, but this is not the case at all. Although all breeders do not advocate crate training, more and more breeders and trainers are recommending crates as a preferred tool for pet puppies as well as show puppies. Crates are not cruel—crates have many humane and highly effective uses in dog care and training. For

Documentation

Two important documents you will get from the breeder are the pup's pedigree and registration papers. The breeder should register the litter and each pup with The Kennel Club, and it is necessary for you to have the paperwork if you plan on showing or breeding in the future.

Make sure you know the breeder's intentions on which type of registration he will obtain for the pup. There are limited registrations which may prohibit the dog from being shown or from competing in non-conformation trials such as Working or Agility if the breeder feels that the pup is not of sufficient quality to do so. There is also a type of registration that will permit the dog in non-conformation competition only.

If your dog is registered with a Kennel-Club-recognised breed club, then you can register the pup with The Kennel Club yourself. Your breeder can assist you with the specifics of the registration process.

You should be prepared with suitable crate, toys, water and food bowls and a few other essentials BEFORE you bring home the English Springer Spaniel.

example, crate training is a very popular and very successful housebreaking method. A crate can keep your dog safe during travel; and, perhaps most importantly, a crate provides your dog with a place of his own in your home. It serves as a 'doggie bedroom' of sorts—your Springer can curl up in his crate when he

Your local pet shop should be the source for all of your pet supplies. Most pet shops have a large variety of crates in all sizes, weights and prices.

wants to sleep or when he just needs a break. Many dogs sleep in their crates overnight. When lined with soft bedding and his favourite toy, a crate becomes a cosy pseudo-den for your dog. Like his ancestors, he too will seek out the comfort and retreat of a den—you just happen to be providing him with something a little more luxurious than his early ancestors enjoyed.

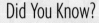

Did You Know?

Unfortunately, when a puppy is bought by someone who does not take into consideration the time and attention that dog ownership requires, it is the puppy who suffers when he is either abandoned or placed in a shelter by a frustrated owner. So all of the 'homework' you do in preparation for your pup's arrival will benefit you both. The more informed you are, the more you will know what to expect and the better equipped you will be to handle the ups and downs of raising a puppy. Hopefully, everyone in the household is willing to do his part in raising and caring for the pup. The anticipation of owning a dog often brings a lot of promises from excited family members: 'I will walk him every day,' 'I will feed him,' 'I will housebreak him,' etc., but these things take time and effort, and promises can easily be forgotten once the novelty of the new pet has worn off.

PHOTO COURTESY OF DOSKOCIL.

As far as purchasing a crate, the type that you buy is up to you. It will likely be one of the two most popular types: wire or fibreglass. There are advantages and disadvantages to each type. For example, a wire crate is more open, allowing the air to flow through and affording the dog a view of what is going on around him whilst a fibreglass crate is sturdier. Both can double as travel crates, providing protection for the dog. The size of the crate is another thing to consider. Puppies do not stay puppies forever—in fact, sometimes it seems as if they grow right before your eyes. A small-sized crate may be fine for a very young Springer pup, but it will not do him much good for long! Unless you have the money and the inclination to buy a new crate every time your pup has a growth spurt, it is better to get one that will accommodate your dog both as a pup and at full size. A medium-size crate will be necessary for a full-grown English Springer Spaniel, who stands approximately 20 inches high.

BEDDING

Veterinary bedding in the dog's crate will help the dog feel more at home and you may also like to pop in a small blanket. This will take the place of the leaves, twigs, etc., that the pup would use in the wild to make a den; the pup can make his own 'burrow' in the crate. Although your pup is far removed from his den-making ancestors, the denning instinct is still a part of his genetic makeup. Second, until you bring your pup home, he has been sleeping amidst the warmth of his mother and littermates, and whilst a blanket is not the same as a warm, breathing body, it still provides heat and something with which to snuggle. You will want to wash your pup's bedding frequently in

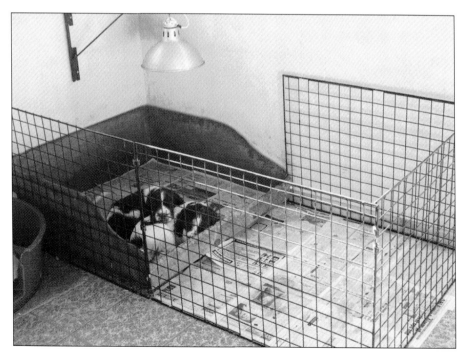

Until you bring your new puppy home, he is used to sleeping amongst the warmth of his littermates.

Puppies need to chew, and they will chew anything! They require safe chew toys to divert their attention from your belongings and items that could be dangerous.

case he has an accident in his crate, and replace or remove any blanket that becomes ragged and starts to fall apart.

Toys

Toys are a must for dogs of all ages, especially for curious playful pups. Puppies are the 'children' of the dog world, and what child does not love toys? Chew toys provide enjoyment to both dog and owner—your dog will enjoy playing with his favourite toys, whilst you will enjoy the fact that they distract him from your expensive shoes and leather sofa. Puppies love to chew; in fact, chewing is a physical need for pups as they are teething, and everything looks appetising! The full range of your possessions—from old dishcloth to Oriental rug—are fair game in the eyes of a teething pup. Puppies are not all that discerning when it comes to finding something to literally 'sink their teeth into'—everything tastes great!

Breeders advise owners to resist stuffed toys, because they can become de-stuffed in no time. The overly excited pup may ingest the stuffing, which is neither digestible nor nutritious.

Tug toys are ideal for puppies because you can initiate a game with your pup as part of the bonding experience. While gentle play with tug toys is good, you should never incite your pup into an aggressive tug-of-war game.

Did You Know?

The majority of problems that are commonly seen in young pups will disappear as your dog gets older. However, how you deal with problems when he is young will determine how he reacts to discipline as an adult dog. It is important to establish who is boss (hopefully it will be you!) right away when you are first bonding with your dog. This bond will set the tone for the rest of your life together.

PHOTO COURTESY OF MIKKI PET PRODUCTS.

Similarly, squeaky toys are quite popular, but if a pup 'disembowels' one of these, the small plastic squeaker inside can be dangerous if swallowed.

Be careful of natural bones, which have a tendency to splinter into sharp, dangerous pieces. Also be careful of rawhide, which can turn into pieces that are easy to swallow or into a mushy mess on your carpet. Most puppies love the calf hooves that you can buy in any pet shop or at shows. They can chew for hours on them without coming to any harm. However, if what's left of the hoof becomes too small you'd better take it away. Monitor the condition of all your pup's toys carefully and get rid of any that have been chewed to the point of becoming potentially dangerous.

LEAD

A nylon lead is probably the best option as it is the most resistant to

Your local pet shop will have a wide variety of leads in many colours, materials and thicknesses. Select a durable lead that will last you and your Springer many years.

puppy teeth. Many a Springer puppy will take a liking to chewing on his lead. Of course, this is a habit that should be 'nipped' in

Photo courtesy of Mikki Pet Products.

Insurance

Many good breeders will offer you insurance with your new puppy, which is an excellent idea. The first few weeks of insurance will probably be covered free of charge or with only minimal cost, allowing you to take up the policy when this expires. If you own a pet dog, it is sensible to take out such a policy as veterinary fees can be high, although routine vaccinations and boosters are not covered. Look carefully at the many options open to you before deciding which suits you best.

There are many high-quality toys made especially for dogs. Only buy toys made for canines, as toys made for human children are not strong enough to withstand puppy teeth.

47

the bud. Nylon leads are strong but lightweight, which is good for a young Springer puppy who is just getting used to the idea of walking on a lead. For everyday walking and safety purposes, the nylon lead is a good choice. As your pup grows up and gets used to walking on the lead, you may want to purchase a flexible lead. These leads allow you to extend the length to give the dog a broader area to explore or to shorten the length to keep the dog close to you. Of course there are special leads for training purposes.

COLLAR

Your pup should get used to wearing a collar all the time since you will want to attach his ID tags to it. A light-weight nylon

> ## Did You Know?
>
> Taking your dog from the breeder to your home in a car can be a very uncomfortable experience for both of you. The puppy will have been taken from his warm, friendly, safe environment and brought into a strange new environment. An environment that moves! Be prepared for loose bowels, urination, crying, whining and even fear biting. With proper love and encouragement when you arrive home, the stress of the trip should quickly disappear.

> ## Did You Know?
>
> The cost of food must also be mentioned. All dogs need a good quality food with an adequate supply of protein to develop their bones and muscles properly. Most dogs are not picky eaters but unless fed properly they can quickly succumb to skin problems.

collar is a good choice. Make sure that it fits snugly enough so that the pup cannot wriggle out of it, but is loose enough so that it will not be uncomfortably tight around the pup's neck. You should be able to fit a finger between the pup and the collar. It may take some time for your pup to get used to wearing the collar, but soon he will not even notice that it is there. Choke collars are made for training, but should only be used by an experienced handler.

FOOD AND WATER BOWLS

Your pup will need two bowls, one for food and one for water. You may want two sets of bowls, one for inside and one for outside, depending on where the dog will be fed and where he will be spending most of his time. Stainless steel bowls that can be sterilised are good, but the sturdy special spaniel bowls whose shape allows the ears to fall outside the bowl are popular choices.

Choose the Right Collar

The BUCKLE COLLAR is the standard collar used for everyday purpose. Be sure that you adjust the buckle on growing puppies. Check it every day. It can become too tight overnight! These collars can be made of leather or nylon. Attach your dog's identification tags to this collar.

Buckle Collar

The CHOKE CHAIN is the usual collar recommended for training. It is constructed of highly polished steel so that it slides easily through the stainless steel loop. The idea is that the dog controls the pressure around its neck and he will stop pulling if the collar becomes uncomfortable. Never leave a choke collar on your dog when not training.

Choke Chain

The HALTER is for a trained dog that has to be restrained to prevent running away, chasing a cat and the like. Considered the most humane of all collars, it is frequently used on smaller dogs for which collars are not comfortable.

Halter

49

Provide your English Springer Spaniel with food and water bowls. These bowls can be constructed of sturdy plastic, ceramic, clay or stainless steel.

PHOTO COURTESY OF MIKKI PET PRODUCTS.

Electrical Fencing

The electrical fencing system which forms an invisible fence works on a battery-operated collar that shocks the dog if it gets too close to the buried (or elevated) wire. There are some people who think very highly of this system of controlling a dog's wandering. Keep in mind that the collar has batteries. For safety's sake, replace the batteries every month with the best quality batteries available.

Did You Know

You should not even think about buying a puppy that looks sick, undernourished, overly frightened or nervous. Sometimes a timid puppy will warm up to you after a 30-minute 'let's-get-acquainted' session.

CLEANING SUPPLIES

Until a pup is housetrained you will be doing a lot of cleaning. Accidents will occur, which is okay in the beginning because the puppy does not know any better. All you can do is be prepared to clean up any 'accidents.' Old rags, towels, newspapers and a safe disinfectant are good to have on hand.

BEYOND THE BASICS

The items previously discussed are the bare necessities. You will find out what else you need as

Responsible, law-abiding dog owners pick up their dogs' droppings whenever they are in public. Pooper-scooper devices make the job quick and easy.

These bowls avoid messy ears after the dinner and a wet floor after drinking! Plastic bowls are very chewable and therefore not advisable. Some dog owners like to put their dogs' food and water bowls on a specially made elevated stand. This brings the food closer to the dog's level so he does not have to bend down as far, thus aiding his digestion and helping to guard against bloat or gastric torsion in deep-chested dogs. The most important thing is to buy sturdy bowls since, again, anything is in danger of being chewed by puppy teeth and you do not want your dog to be constantly chewing apart his bowl (for his safety and for your wallet!).

Crate Training Tips

During crate training, you should partition off the section of the crate in which the pup stays. If he is given too big an area, this will hinder your training efforts. Crate training is based on the fact that a dog does not like to soil his sleeping quarters, so it is ineffective to keep a pup in a crate that is so big that he can eliminate in one end and get far enough away from it to sleep. Also, you want to make the crate den-like for the pup. Blankets and a favourite toy will make the crate cosy for the small pup; as he grows, you may want to evict some of his 'roommates' to make more room.

It will take some coaxing at first, but be patient. Given some time to get used to it, your pup will adapt to his new home-within-a-home quite nicely.

you go along—grooming supplies, flea/tick protection, baby gates to partition a room, etc. These things will vary depending on your situation but it is important that you have everything you need to feed and make your Springer comfortable in his first few days at home.

PUPPY-PROOFING YOUR HOME
Aside from making sure that your English Springer Spaniel will be comfortable in your home, you also have to make sure that your home is safe for your Springer. This means taking precautions that your pup will not get into anything he should not and that there is nothing within his reach that may harm him should he sniff it, chew it, inspect it, etc. This probably seems obvious since, whilst you are primarily concerned with your pup's safety, at the same time you do not want your belongings to be ruined. Breakables should be placed out

An average home contains many potential dangers for a curious pup...a fireplace is just one example. The house should be puppy-proofed BEFORE bringing the pup home, and constant supervision is necessary.

Natural Toxins

Examine your lawn and garden landscaping before bringing your puppy home. Many varieties of plants have leaves, stems or flowers that are toxic if ingested, and you can depend on a curious puppy to investigate them. Ask your vet for information on poisonous plants or research them at your library.

of reach if your dog is to have full run of the house. If he is to be limited to certain places within the house, keep any potentially dangerous items in the 'off-limits' areas. An electrical cord can pose a danger should the puppy decide

Training Tip

Training your puppy takes much patience and can be frustrating at times, but you should see results from your efforts. If you have a puppy that seems untrainable, take him to a trainer or behaviourist. The dog may have a personality problem that requires the help of a professional, or perhaps you need help in learning how to train your dog.

to taste it—and who is going to convince a pup that it would not make a great chew toy? Cords should be fastened tightly against the wall. If your dog is going to spend time in a crate, make sure that there is nothing near his crate that he can reach if he sticks his curious little nose or paws through the openings. Just as you would with a child, keep all household cleaners and chemicals where the pup cannot get to them.

It is also important to make sure that the outside of your home is safe. Of course your puppy should never be unsupervised, but a pup let loose in the garden will want to run and explore, and he should be granted that freedom. Do not let a fence give you a false sense of security; you would be surprised how crafty (and persistent) a dog can be in figuring out how to dig under and squeeze his way through small holes, or to jump or climb over a fence. The remedy is to make the fence high enough so that it really is impossible for your dog to get over it (about 3 metres should suffice), and well embedded into the ground. Be sure to repair or secure any gaps in the fence. Check the fence periodically to ensure that it is in good shape and make repairs as needed; a very determined pup may return to the same spot to 'work on it' until he is able to get through.

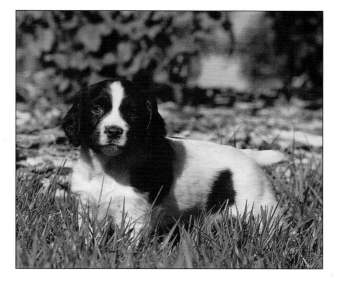

FIRST TRIP TO THE VET
You have picked out your puppy, and your home and family are ready. Now all you have to do is collect your English Springer Spaniel from the breeder and the fun begins, right? Well…not so fast. Something else you need to prepare is your pup's first trip to

An active Springer pup will love to spend time running and playing in the garden, so make sure that the garden is safe for the puppy.

Toxic Plants

Many plants can be toxic to dogs. If you see your dog carrying a piece of vegetation in his mouth, approach him in a quiet, disinterested manner, avoid eye contact, pet him and gradually remove the plant from his mouth. Alternatively, offer him a treat and maybe he'll drop the plant on his own accord. Be sure no toxic plants are growing in your own garden.

53

the veterinary surgeon. Perhaps the breeder can recommend someone in the area that specialises in Springer Spaniels, or maybe you know some other Springer Spaniel owners who can suggest a good vet. Either way, you should have an appointment arranged for your pup before you pick him up and plan on taking him for an examination before bringing him home.

The pup's first visit will consist of an overall examination to make sure that the pup does not have any problems that are not apparent to the eye. The veterinary surgeon will also set up a schedule for the pup's vaccinations; the breeder will inform you of which ones the pup has already received and the vet can continue from there.

INTRODUCTION TO THE FAMILY

Everyone in the house will be excited about the puppy coming home and will want to pet him and play with him, but it is best to make the introduction low-key so as not to overwhelm the puppy. He is apprehensive already. It is the first time he has been separated from his mother and the breeder, and the ride to your home is likely the first time he has been in a car. The last thing you want to do is smother him, as this will only frighten him further. This is not to say that human contact is not extremely necessary at this stage, because this is the time when a connection between the pup and his human family is formed. Gentle petting and soothing words should help console him, as well as just putting him down and letting him explore on his own (under your watchful eye, of course).

The pup may approach the family members or may busy himself with exploring for a while. Gradually, each person should spend some time with the pup, one at a time, crouching down to get as close to the pup's level as possible and letting him sniff their hands and petting him gently. He definitely needs human attention and he needs to be touched—this is how to form an immediate bond. Just remember that the pup is experiencing a lot of things for the first time, at the same time. There are new people, new noises, new smells, and new things to investigate: so be gentle, be affectionate, and be as comforting as you can.

Chemical Toxins

Scour your carport for potential puppy dangers. Remove weed killers, pesticides and antifreeze materials. Antifreeze is highly toxic and even a few drops can kill an adult dog. The sweet taste attracts the animal, who will quickly consume it from the floor or curbside.

Puppy-proofing

Thoroughly puppy-proof your house before bringing your puppy home. Never use roach or rodent poisons in any area accessible to the puppy. Avoid the use of toilet bowl cleaners. Most dogs are born with toilet bowl sonar and will take a drink if the lid is left open. Also keep the trash secured and out of reach.

YOUR PUP'S FIRST NIGHT HOME

You have travelled home with your new charge safely in his basket or crate. He's been to the vet for a thorough check-over; he's been weighed, his papers examined; perhaps he's even been vaccinated and wormed as well. He's met the family, licked the whole family, including the excited children and the less-than-happy cat. He's explored his area, his new

Even very young children should be taught to treat pets with care and respect. A child who grows up around dogs will naturally accept them as part of the family.

These Springer pups have a great opportunity for socialisation with their dam, littermates, other dogs and people of different ages.

bed, the garden and anywhere else he's been permitted. He's eaten his first meal at home and relieved himself in the proper place. He's heard lots of new sounds, smelled new friends and seen more of the outside world than ever before.

That was just the first day! He's worn out and is ready for bed...or so you think!

It's puppy's first night and you are ready to say 'Good night'— keep in mind that this is puppy's first night ever to be sleeping alone. His dam and littermates are no longer at paw's length and he's a bit scared, cold and lonely. Be reassuring to your new family member. This is not the time to spoil him and give in to his inevitable whining.

Puppies whine. They whine to let the others know where they

Did You Know?

You will probably start feeding your pup the same food that he has been getting from the breeder; the breeder should give you a few days' supply to start you off. Although you should not give your pup too many treats, you will want to have puppy treats on hand for coaxing, training, rewards, etc. Be careful, though, as a small pup's calorie requirements are relatively low and a few treats can add up to almost a full day's worth of calories without the required nutrition.

are and hopefully to get company out of it. Place your pup in his new bed or crate in his room and close the door. Mercifully, he may fall asleep without a peep. If the inevitable occurs, ignore the whining: he is fine. Be strong and keep his interest in mind. Do not allow your heart to become guilty and visit the pup. He will fall asleep.

Many breeders recommend placing a piece of bedding from his former homestead in his new bed so that he recognises the scent of his littermates. Others still advise placing a hot water bottle in his bed for warmth. This latter may be a good idea provided the pup doesn't attempt to suckle—he'll get good and wet and may not fall asleep so fast.

Puppy's first night can be somewhat stressful for the pup and his new family. Remember that you are setting the tone of nighttime at your house. Unless you want to play with your pup every evening at 10 p.m., midnight and 2 a.m., don't initiate the habit. Your family will thank you, and so will your pup!

PREVENTING PUPPY PROBLEMS

SOCIALISATION

Now that you have done all of the preparatory work and have helped your pup get accustomed to his new home and family, it is about time for you to have some fun! Socialising your English Springer Spaniel pup gives you the opportunity to show off your new friend, and your pup gets to reap the benefits of being an adorable furry creature that people will want to pet and, in general, think is absolutely precious!

Besides getting to know his new family, your puppy should be exposed to other people, animals and situations, but of course he must not come into close contact with dogs you don't know well until his course of injections is fully complete. This will help him become well adjusted as he grows up and less prone to being timid or fearful of the new things he will encounter. Your pup's socialisation began at the breeder's but now it is your responsibility to continue it. The socialisation he receives up until the age of 12 weeks is the most critical, as this is the time when he forms his impressions of the outside world. Be especially careful during the eight-to-ten-week period, also known as the fear period. The interaction he receives during this time should be gentle and reassuring. Lack of socialisation can manifest itself in fear and aggression as the dog grows up. He needs lots of human contact, affection, handling and exposure

Financial Responsibility

Grooming tools, collars, leashes, dog beds and, of course, toys will be an expense to you when you first obtain your pup, and the cost will trickle on throughout your dog's lifetime. If your puppy damages or destroys your possessions (as most puppies surely will!) or something belonging to a neighbour, you can calculate additional expense. There is also flea and pest control, which every dog owner faces more than once. You must be able to handle the financial responsibility of owning a dog.

to other animals.

Once your pup has received his necessary vaccinations, feel free to take him out and about (on his lead, of course). Walk him around the neighbourhood, take him on your daily errands, let people pet him, let him meet other dogs and pets, etc. Puppies do not have to try to make friends; there will be no shortage of people who will want to introduce themselves. Just make sure that you carefully supervise each meeting. If the neighbourhood children want to say hello, for example, that is great—children and pups most often make great companions. Sometimes an excited child can unintentionally handle a pup too roughly, or an overzealous pup can playfully nip a little too hard. You want to

Socialisation

Thorough socialisation includes not only meeting new people but also being introduced to new experiences such as riding in the car, having his coat brushed, hearing the television, walking in a crowd—the list is endless. The more your pup experiences, and the more positive the experiences are, the less of a shock and the less scary it will be for your pup to encounter new things.

make socialisation experiences positive ones. What a pup learns during this very formative stage will impact his attitude toward future encounters. You want your dog to be comfortable around everyone. A pup that has a bad experience with a child may grow up to be a dog that is shy around or aggressive toward children.

CONSISTENCY IN TRAINING

Dogs, being pack animals, naturally need a leader, or else they try to establish dominance in their packs. When you bring a dog into your family, the choice of who becomes the leader and who becomes the 'pack' is entirely up to you! Your pup's intuitive quest for dominance, coupled with the fact that it is nearly impossible to look at an adorable Springer Spaniel pup, with his 'puppy-dog' eyes and his floppy ears, and not cave in, give the pup almost an unfair advantage in getting the upper hand! A pup will definitely test the waters to see what he can and cannot do. Do not give in to those pleading eyes—stand your ground when it comes to disciplining the pup and make sure that all family members do the same. It will only confuse the pup when Mother tells him to get off the couch when he is used to sitting up there with Father to watch the nightly news. Avoid discrepancies by having all members of the

If you don't want your Springer(s) on the furniture, enforce the rules early on. Otherwise, you may find that your favourite spot on the sofa has 'gone to the dogs!'

household decide on the rules before the pup even comes home…and be consistent in enforcing them! Early training shapes the dog's personality, so you cannot be unclear in what you expect.

COMMON PUPPY PROBLEMS
The best way to prevent puppy problems is to be proactive in stopping an undesirable behaviour as soon as it starts. The old saying 'You can't teach an old dog new tricks' does not necessarily hold true, but it is true that it is much easier to discourage bad behaviour in a young developing pup than to

wait until the pup's bad behaviour becomes the adult dog's bad habit. There are some problems that are especially prevalent in puppies as they develop.

Did You Know?

It will take at least two weeks for your puppy to become accustomed to his new surroundings. Give him lots of love, attention, handling, frequent opportunities to relieve himself, a diet he likes to eat and a place he can call his own.

59

NIPPING

As puppies start to teethe, they feel the need to sink their teeth into anything available…unfortunately that includes your

Chewing Tips

Chewing goes hand in hand with nipping in the sense that a teething puppy is always looking for a way to soothe his aching gums. In this case, instead of chewing on you, he may have taken a liking to your favourite shoe or something else which he should not be chewing. Again, realise that this is a normal canine behaviour that does not need to be discouraged, only redirected. Your pup just needs to be taught what is acceptable to chew on and what is off limits. Consistently tell him NO when you catch him chewing on something forbidden and give him a chew toy. Conversely, praise him when you catch him chewing on something appropriate. In this way you are discouraging the inappropriate behaviour and reinforcing the desired behaviour. The puppy chewing should stop after his adult teeth have come in, but an adult dog continues to chew for various reasons—perhaps because he is bored, perhaps to relieve tension or perhaps he just likes to chew. That is why it is important to redirect his chewing when he is still young.

fingers, arms, hair and toes. You may find this behaviour cute for the first five seconds…until you feel just how sharp those puppy teeth are. This is something you want to discourage immediately and consistently with a firm 'No!' (or whatever number of firm 'No's' it takes for him to understand that you mean business). Then replace your finger with an appropriate chew toy. Whilst this behaviour is merely annoying when the dog is young, it can become highly unpleasant as your Springer Spaniel's adult teeth grow in and his jaws develop, and he continues to think it is okay to gnaw on human appendages. Your Springer Spaniel does not mean any harm with a friendly nip, but he also does not know his own strength.

CRYING/WHINING

Your pup will often cry, whine, whimper, howl or make some type of commotion when he is left alone. This is basically his way of calling out for attention to make sure that you know he is there and that you have not forgotten about him. He feels insecure when he is left alone, when you are out of the house and he is in his crate or when you are in another part of the house and he cannot see you. The noise he is making is an expression of the anxiety he feels at being alone, so he needs to be taught that being alone is okay. You are not actually training the dog to stop making noise, you are training him to feel comfortable when he is alone and thus removing the need for him to make the noise. This is where the crate filled with cosy bedding and a toy comes in handy. You want to know that he is safe when you are not there to supervise, and you know that he will be safe in his crate rather than roaming freely about the house. In order for the pup to stay in his crate without making a fuss, he needs to be comfortable in his crate. On that note, it is extremely important that the

Springers love the great outdoors, no matter the weather. This pup looks like he's enjoyed his first encounter with snow.

Whether you intend to hunt with your Springer or just enjoy him as a pet, the English Springer Spaniel makes a wonderful companion for the right owners.

crate is never used as a form of punishment, or the pup will have a negative association with the crate.

Accustom the pup to the crate in short, gradually increasing time intervals in which you put him in the crate, maybe with a treat, and stay in the room with him. If he cries or makes a fuss, do not go to him, but stay in his sight. Gradually he will realise that staying in his crate is all right without your help, and it will not be so traumatic for him when you are not around. You may want to leave the radio on softly when you leave the house; the sound of human voices may be comforting to him.

DIETARY AND FEEDING CONSIDERATIONS

Today the choices of food for your English Springer Spaniel are many and varied. There are simply dozens of brands of food in all sorts of flavours and textures, ranging from puppy diets to those for seniors. There are even hypoallergenic and low-calorie diets available. Because your English Springer Spaniel's food has a bearing on coat, health and temperament, it is essential that the most suitable diet be selected for a dog of his age. It is fair to say, however, that even dedicated owners can be somewhat perplexed by the enormous range of foods available. Only understanding what is best for your dog will help you reach a valued decision.

There are four basic types of dog foods: fresh, preferably raw meat; dried food; semi-moist food; and canned or tinned meat. For meat the most commonly used is tripe, and dogs love it. You can combine their meat meals with dried food or with a semi-moist meal or, if fresh meat is not available, with tinned meat. Dried foods are useful for the cost-conscious for overall they tend to be less expensive than semi-moist or tinned, but dogs often get bored with them. How would you feel if you had the same meal day after day, year after year? Dried food contains the least fat and the most preservatives. In general tinned

Food Preference

Selecting the best dried dog food is difficult. There is no majority consensus amongst veterinary scientists as to the value of nutrient analyses (protein, fat, fibre, moisture, ash, cholesterol, minerals, etc.). All agree that feeding trials are what matters, but you also have to consider the individual dog. Its weight, age, activity and what pleases its taste all must be considered. It is probably best to take the advice of your veterinary surgeon. Every dog's dietary requirements vary, even during the lifetime of a particular dog.

If your dog is fed a good dried food, it does not require supplements of meat or vegetables. Dogs do appreciate a little variety in their diets so you may choose to stay with the same brand, but vary the flavour. Alternatively you may wish to add a little flavoured stock to give a difference to the taste.

A well-balanced puppy food will provide your young Springer with the nutrition he needs to grow up healthy.

foods are made up of 60–70 percent water, whilst semi-moist ones often contain so much sugar that they are perhaps the least pre-

Did You Know?

A good test for proper diet is the colour, odour, and firmness of your dog's stool. A healthy dog usually produces three semi-hard stools per day. The stools should have no unpleasant odour. They should be the same colour from excretion to excretion.

ferred by owners, even though their dogs seem to like them. Most dogs love vegetables and fruit and it certainly doesn't do them any harm to surprise them with a quarter of an apple, some leftover runner beans or lettuce.

When selecting your dog's diet, three stages of development must be considered: the puppy stage, adult stage and the senior or veteran stage.

PUPPY STAGE
Puppies instinctively want to suck milk from their mother's teats and

a normal puppy will exhibit this behaviour from just a few moments following birth. If puppies do not attempt to suckle within the first half-hour or so, they should be encouraged to do so by placing them on the nipples, having selected ones with plenty of milk. This early milk supply is important in providing colostrum to protect the puppies during the first eight to ten weeks of their lives. Although a mother's milk is much better than any milk formula, despite there being

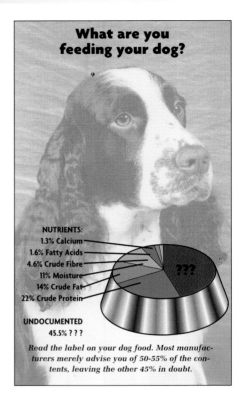

What are you feeding your dog?

NUTRIENTS:
1.3% Calcium
1.6% Fatty Acids
4.6% Crude Fibre
11% Moisture
14% Crude Fat
22% Crude Protein

???

UNDOCUMENTED
45.5% ? ? ?

Read the label on your dog food. Most manufacturers merely advise you of 50-55% of the contents, leaving the other 45% in doubt.

Did You Know?

Dog food must be at room temperature, neither too hot nor too cold. Fresh water, changed daily and served in a clean bowl, is mandatory, especially when feeding dried food.

Never feed your dog from the table while you are eating. This encourages the dog to beg at the table. He should have a designated area in which to eat.

Dogs must chew their food. Hard pellets are excellent; soups and slurries are to be avoided.

Don't add supplements to normal dog food unless advised by the vet. The normal food is usually balanced and adding something extra destroys the balance.

Except for age-related changes, dogs do not require dietary variations to receive complete nutrition if they are fed a balanced dog food.

some excellent ones available, if the puppies do not feed you will have to feed them yourself. For those with less experience, advice from a veterinary surgeon is important so that you feed not only the right quantity of milk but that of correct quality, fed at suitably frequent intervals, usually every two hours during the first few days of life.

Puppies should be allowed to nurse from their mothers for about the first six weeks, although from the third or fourth week you will have begun to introduce small

This Springer litter is certainly keeping mother busy! Their mother's milk is critical and necessary for the pups for their first six weeks.

portions of suitable solid food. Most breeders like to introduce alternate milk and meat meals initially, building up to weaning time.

By the time the puppies are seven or a maximum of eight weeks old, they should be fully weaned and fed solely on a proprietary puppy food. Selection of the most suitable, good-quality diet at this time is essential for a puppy's fastest growth rate is during the first year of life. Veterinary surgeons are usually able to offer advice in this

regard and, although the frequency of meals will have been reduced over time, only when a young dog has reached the age of about 18 months should an adult diet be fed.

Did You Know?

You must store your dried dog food carefully. Open packages of dog food quickly lose their vitamin value, usually within 90 days of being opened. Mould spores and vermin could also contaminate the food.

Puppy and junior diets should be well balanced for the needs of your dog, so that except in certain circumstances additional vitamins, minerals and proteins will not be required.

When you decided to buy your puppy, the breeder probably told you what you have to feed the puppy once you bring him home. If he didn't, ask him. This is important for two reasons: coming to live with you in totally new surroundings with so many new experiences is already a stressful experience for the puppy and a continuation of his diet will help him. Even then his tummy may be upset the first couple of days, or he may even refuse to eat for a day or two, but don't worry about that. As soon as he is settled down he will eat again, especially if it's the food he has been used to. Also, the breeder most likely has a lot of experience in feeding mature dogs and puppies and keeping them in a peak condition, so it would be wise to listen to his advice. Most breeders will provide you with an exact list of what to feed the puppy at which stage of his life and we strongly advise you to follow these instructions. Once your puppy is a mature one or two year old, you can change his diet to what is more convenient for you (availability, costs, etc.), but with the growing puppy and youngster, stay with the breeder's diet. And remember that if ten breeders are discussing the feeding of their dogs, you will hear ten different opinions, and all of them will be right!

Your puppy will need three or four meals a day until he is about nine months old, then you can cut back to two daily meals. Some people prefer to feed the adult dog once a day but if your dog loves his food, he probably won't go along with that! He might prefer to have a breakfast and a dinner.

Grain-based Diets

Many adult diets are based on grain. There is nothing wrong with this as long as it does not contain soy meal. Diets based on soy often cause flatulence (passing gas).

Grain-based diets are almost always the least expensive and a good grain diet is just as good as the most expensive diet containing animal protein.

There are many cases, however, when your dog might require a special diet. These special requirements should only be recommended by your veterinary surgeon.

ADULT DIETS

A dog is considered an adult when it has stopped growing. The growth is in height and/or length. Do not consider the dog's weight when the decision is made to switch from a puppy diet to a maintenance diet. Again you

SENIOR DIETS

As dogs get older, their metabolism changes. The older dog usually exercises less, moves more slowly and sleeps more. This change in lifestyle and physiological performance requires a change in diet. Since these changes take place slowly, they might not be recognisable. What is easily recognisable is weight gain. By continuing to feed your dog an adult-maintenance diet when it is slowing down metabolically, your dog will gain weight. Obesity in an older dog compounds the health problems that already accompany old age. So here as well, feed 'with your eyes.'

As your dog gets older, few of their organs function up to par. The kidneys slow down and the intestines become less efficient. These age-related factors are best handled with a change in diet and a change in feeding schedule to give smaller portions that are more easily digested.

There is no single best diet for every older dog. Whilst many dogs do well on light or senior diets, other dogs do better on puppy diets or other special premium diets such as lamb and rice. Be sensitive to your senior English Springer Spaniel's diet and this will help control other problems that may arise with your old friend.

Once your Springer stops growing, he can begin an adult maintenance diet. A nutritionally complete adult diet will likely suffice for the rest of the dog's life unless otherwise indicated by the vet.

should rely on your breeder's advice. A Springer Spaniel reaches adulthood at about two years of age, though some dogs are fully mature at 18 months whilst others may take up to three years.

Major dog food manufacturers specialise in maintenance diets, and it is just necessary for you to select the one best suited to your dog's needs. Whatever you are going to feed your dog don't rely entirely on the quantities given in the manufacturer's instructions. Every dog has different requirements, active dogs may have different requirements than sedate dogs and—as in humans—where one dog will grow fat on just a small portion, another will need double the quantity. So it is best to 'feed with your eyes.'

67

Swimming may be the Springer's favourite activity. If there's water around, your Springer will try his hardest to dive in!

WATER

Just as your dog needs proper nutrition from his food, water is an essential 'nutrient' as well. Water keeps the dog's body properly hydrated and promotes normal function of the body's systems. During housebreaking it is necessary to keep an eye on how much water your English Springer Spaniel is drinking, but once he is reliably trained he should have access to clean fresh water at all times. Make sure that the dog's water bowl is clean, and change the water often, making sure that water is always available for your dog, especially if you feed dried food.

You will find that your Springer Spaniel is a very sloppy drinker: he loves his water bowl and in his enthusiasm he will often put not only his mouth but also both front paws in the bowl. Or he will take one last mouthfull of water and before swallowing it come to you to tell you how much he loves you! A special spaniel bowl may help you keep the kitchen floor clean.

EXERCISE

All dogs require some form of exercise, regardless of breed. A sedentary lifestyle is as harmful to a dog as it is to a person. The Springer Spaniel is a very lively and active breed that requires a lot of free exercise. He might like to come with you on a shopping expedition but what he needs is to run around free, preferably in exciting surroundings, like woods or fields, where he can develop his hunting instincts.

Owners often make mistakes in the exercise they give their dog. Whereas the new puppy is an exciting thing, they tend to give too much exercise. It is only human to show off with something you are very proud of, but it means that the small puppy is taken on too many walks. For a puppy up to six months, the garden is big enough. Provided he is properly inoculated, take him to the park once a day to let him socialise and play with the other dogs for about 15 minutes. Once the puppy is about nine months old, you can extend the daily walks to an hour daily and once he is a year old his energy will be boundless.

We cannot stress the importance of exercise enough. It is essential to keep the dog's body fit, but it is also essential to his mental well being. A bored dog will find something to do, which often manifests itself in some type of destructive behaviour. In this sense, it is essential for your mental well being as well!

GROOMING
BRUSHING
A natural bristle brush or a slicker brush can be used for regular routine brushing. Daily brushing is effective for removing dead hair and stimulating the dog's natural oils to add shine and a healthy look to the coat. Also, the soft and silky spaniel coat can easily form tangles and matts, especially in places like the armpits and behind the ears and it is important to prevent these from forming.

TRIMMING AND PRESENTATION
When you buy your puppy, it will have a smooth, short coat without much feathering, but by the time your puppy is five or six months old, you'll find that fluffy puppy hair starts growing on his head and throat, his feet and his legs and on his markings. Your dog will have lost his shiny coat but don't worry, this doesn't mean he is not healthy! It is just his puppy coat, which he will grow out of in due time.

The English Springer Spaniel's coat is flat, straight and silky, without waves or curls. The best way to shape the coat is by hand-plucking. You may prefer

The Springer requires regular brushing to keep his coat neat and matt-free.

Grooming Equipment

How much grooming equipment you purchase will depend on how much grooming you are going to do. Here are some basics:
- Natural bristle brush
- Slicker brush
- Thumblettes
- Trimming blade
- Metal comb
- Scissors
- Blaster
- Rubber mat
- Dog shampoo
- Spray hose attachment
- Ear cleaner
- Cotton wipes
- Towels
- Nail clippers

Keeping the hair on the foot and between the pads neatly trimmed should be part of your Springer's regular grooming routine.

the fact that what you want is a show trim. Your Springer must be shaped in the model in which he looks his best and, again, this should be done by hand-plucking and not by scissoring or clippering.

The puppy's coat may take some time to get ready to come out; sometimes you have to wait until the puppy is eight or nine months old. This is annoying when you want to show the puppy, but be patient! Don't hurry the coat by using cutting instruments; you will regret that later.

What you should do in the meantime is groom your puppy regularly so that it is quite used to being on a table and being handled. Also the abundant hair around the feet, between the pads

using thumblettes or surgical gloves to get a better grip but resist the temptation of using the thinning scissors as long as possible. Clipping and razoring are absolutely out of the question since they destroy the density of colour and you will never get that lovely, silky sheen that you get when you handtrim the coat.

If you think you are not up to this job, you'll have to seek help. Ask the breeder whether he can help you. Some breeders use their (little) spare time to trim. If not, you'll have to take your puppy to a professional trimmer. Be very careful where you go, since grooming parlours often believe that their canine clients want nothing but having all of their 'excess hair' removed. For the lovely Springer, that means that the featherings on his legs go, his back is clippered and the beautiful feathering on the ears is cut off. You have to stress on the underside and at the inside of the ear around the ear opening can be cut away.

When you find that your puppy's coat is ready to come out, you may find it easier to remove the hair by using thumblettes, which fit over your thumb and forefinger, or thin surgical gloves, which are quite tight fitting.

Other equipment you may need includes a fine-toothed metal comb with short teeth (or a flea comb), a wider toothed long-bladed comb, a pair of scissors as used by a hairdresser, a pair of thinning scissors with one normal blade and one blade with fine teeth, and a trimming blade.

Start with the head. Gently pull out the long hair on top of

Your Springer's teeth need attention, too. Pet shops will sell toothbrushes and toothpaste made especially for dogs.

the skull, always pulling in the direction the hair grows. This sounds painful, but it is not, since what you pull out is dead hair. Start with just a couple of hairs so that your puppy can get used to the feel and you won't run the risk of hurting him by pulling out too many hairs at the same time. If you have a really smooth finish on top of the head, go to the top of the ears and remove the long hairs there, shaping around the back of the ear and about one-third on the way down. You might use the trimming blade here if you cannot manage with the thumblettes.

With your thinning scissors, cut carefully under the corner of the ear next to the head and the inside of the ear. Vets will often tell you that spaniels always have ear problems. This is not true. As long as you keep the inside of the ear clean and free of hair so that the ear can 'breathe' and, if necessary, use ear cleaner, you'll find that your Springer's ears do not have problems.

Rubber thumblettes are used to pluck hairs that are starting to moult.

Next, thin out all the long and surplus hair from the breastbone up to and including the throat. Don't forget the underside of the lower jaw and the inside of the lipfolds. Make the hair very short here.

The neck must be trimmed out as short as possible, also with finger and thumb. If you have used the fine comb regularly, you'll find that it will have removed nearly all the puppy fluff. Try to use the comb as a stripper by gripping the hair between the comb and your thumb and pulling it towards you. It helps when you weave an elastic band between the teeth of the comb. Make a smooth transition from throat and chest to shoulder blades with the thinning scissors.

Scenes from a grooming session: (top) hand plucking, (middle) trimming hair on the ears and (bottom) using a fine-toothed comb.

Continue down the shoulders until they are smooth and clear. The forelegs may have some fluffy hair on the sides and the front. This must be removed. The feathering at the backside of the front legs stays as it is. The feathering should not touch the ground; when it does you can shape it with the scissors. When viewed from the front, the feathering should lie backwards quite naturally from the elbow.

Work the comb with the elastic band through the body coat, the hair on the ribs and on the outside of the hindlegs. Pluck the fluffy hair that won't come out with the comb. Leave the feathering on the front and back but remove the fluffy hair on the side. Shape the hair on the hock with the thinning scissors.

Trim the tail and cut underneath it. Pluck the hair down to where the feathering falls downwards and trim the feathering into shape.

Trimming the feet is not easy and you have to be very careful. Start with lifting the foot and cutting out all the surplus hair from underneath. Cut closely around the outline of the foot. Then put the foot down and cut the surplus hair away that sticks up between the toes with the thinning scissors. Cut in the direction of the toes. Do not cut the hair between the toes away, since that makes the foot look like a splayed foot. Finish off with a good brush and your Springer is now a picture of health and condition.

BATHING

Dogs do not need to be bathed as often as humans, but sometimes a bath will be necessary. It is therefore important that you accustom your pup to being bathed as a puppy, so that he is used to it when he grows up. You will have to bathe your dog the day before a show and most owners like to bathe their bitches after they have been in season.

Before you bathe your dog, check the coat for tangles. Make sure that your dog has a good

Scenes from a grooming session: (top) trimming the tail, (middle) trimming hair between the foot pads and (bottom) trimming hair on the muzzle.

Bathing the Springer: (top) thoroughly wet the coat before shampooing, (middle) towel drying to remove excess water and (bottom) finishing with a blaster.

non-slip surface to stand on. Begin by wetting the dog's coat. A shower or hose attachment is necessary for thoroughly wetting and rinsing the coat. Check the water temperature to make sure that it is neither too hot nor too cold. Fill his ear openings with cotton wool so that there is no chance of water or soap coming into the ear canals. (Don't forget to remove it after the bath.)

Next, apply shampoo to the dog's coat and work it into a good lather. You should purchase a shampoo that is made for dogs; do not use a product made for human hair. Wash the head last; you do not want shampoo to drip into the dog's eyes whilst you are washing the rest of his body. Work the shampoo all the way down to the skin. You can use this opportunity to check the skin for

Did You Know?

The use of human soap products like shampoo, bubble bath and hand soap can be damaging to a dog's coat and skin. Human products are too strong and remove the protective oils coating the dog's hair and skin (making him water-resistant). Use only shampoo made especially for dogs and you may like to use a medicated shampoo, which will always help to keep external parasites at bay.

any bumps, bites or other abnormalities. Do not neglect any area of the body—get all of the hard-to-reach places.

Once the dog has been thoroughly shampooed, he requires an equally thorough rinsing. Shampoo left in the coat can become irritating to the skin. Protect his eyes from the shampoo by shielding them with your hand and directing the flow of water in the opposite direction.

Be prepared for your dog to shake out his coat—you might want to stand back, but make sure you have a hold on the dog to keep him from running through the house.

(Top) Trimming nails with a 'guillotine'-type clipper, (middle) cleaning ears and (bottom) scaling teeth, which is usually done by the vet.

Grooming Tip

Once you are sure that the dog is thoroughly rinsed, squeeze the excess water out of the coat with your hand and dry him with a heavy towel. You may choose to use a blaster on his coat or just let it dry naturally. In cold weather, never allow your dog outside with a wet coat.

There are 'dry bath' products on the market, which are sprays and powders intended for spot cleaning, that can be used between regular baths, if necessary. They are not substitutes for regular baths, but they are easy to use for touch-ups as they do not require rinsing.

EAR CLEANING

The ears should be kept clean and any excess hair inside the ear should be trimmed. Ears can be cleaned with wipes made especially for dogs and especially for this purpose. Be on the lookout for any signs of infections or ear-mite infestation and during the summer for grass-seeds that may be picked up from the grass by the ears and find their way into the ear canal. If your English Springer Spaniel has been shaking his head or scratching at his ears frequently, this usually indicates a problem. Don't clean the ear canal yourself. If you poke into the ear canal with pincers and cotton wool, you'll only succeed in aggravating things. Contact your vet before the condition gets serious. If his ears have an unusual odour, this is a sure sign of mite infestation or infection, and a signal to have his ears checked by the veterinary surgeon.

If you check your spaniel's ears regularly and use the ear wipes when the ear doesn't look a 100% clean, you will find that the spaniel's reputation for ear-trouble is totally unfounded.

NAIL CLIPPING

Your Springer should be accustomed to having his nails trimmed at an early age, since it will be part of your maintenance routine throughout his life. Not only does it look nicer but also a dog with long nails can cause injury if he jumps up or if he scratches someone unintentionally. Also, a long nail has a better chance of ripping and bleeding, or causing feet to spread. A good rule of thumb is that if you can hear your dog's nails clicking on the floor when he walks, his nails are too long.

Before you start cutting make sure you can identify the 'quick' in each nail. The quick is a blood vessel that runs through the centre of each nail and grows rather close to the end. It will bleed profusely if accidentally cut, which will be quite painful for the dog as it contains nerve endings. Keep some type of clotting agent on hand, such as a styptic pencil or styptic powder (the type used for shaving). This will stop the bleeding quickly when applied to the end of the cut nail. Do not panic if this happens, just stop the bleed-

Did You Know?

A dog that spends a lot of time outside on a hard surface, such as cement or pavement, will have his nails naturally worn down and may not need to have them trimmed as often, except maybe in the colder months when he is not outside as much. Regardless, it is best to get your dog accustomed to this procedure at an early age so that he is used to it. Some dogs are especially sensitive about having their feet touched, but if a dog has experienced it since he was young, he should not be bothered by it.

ing and talk soothingly to your dog. Once he has calmed down, move on to the next nail. It is better to clip a little at a time, particularly with black-nailed dogs.

Hold your pup steady as you begin trimming his nails; you do not want him to make any sudden movements or jump off the table. Talk to him soothingly and stroke his fur as you clip. Holding his foot in your hand, simply take off the end of each nail in one quick clip. You can purchase nail clippers that are specially made for dogs; you can probably find them wherever you buy pet or grooming supplies. You may find the 'guillotine' type the best ones to use.

If you feel all this is beyond you, you might prefer the use of a nail grinder. This is a small, battery-operated appliance that slowly grinds the nails. There is no fear of cutting into the quick and most dogs don't mind the buzzing sound of the grinder at all.

TRAVELLING WITH YOUR DOG
CAR TRAVEL

You should accustom your English Springer Spaniel to riding in a car at an early age. If you are lucky, the breeder has already taken the puppies in his car for a visit to the vet or just for a ride, so that when you come to take your puppy home he knows what it is to be in a car. You will find that most Springers love a ride in the car.

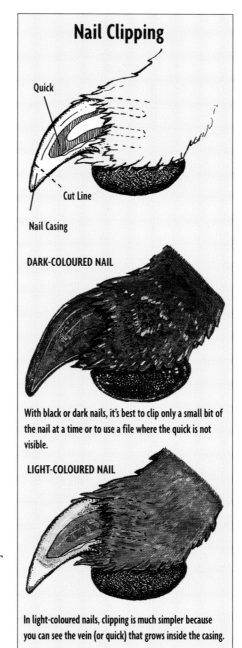

Nail Clipping

Quick

Cut Line

Nail Casing

DARK-COLOURED NAIL

With black or dark nails, it's best to clip only a small bit of the nail at a time or to use a file where the quick is not visible.

LIGHT-COLOURED NAIL

In light-coloured nails, clipping is much simpler because you can see the vein (or quick) that grows inside the casing.

Your local pet shop will have a large supply of grooming tools that you can use on your English Springer Spaniel.

PHOTO COURTESY OF MIKKI PET PRODUCTS.

The best way for a dog to travel in a car is in his crate. You can use either the fibreglass or the wire crates. Another option is the specially made safety harness for dogs, which straps the dog in much like a seat belt. Do not let the dog roam loose in the vehicle—this is very dangerous! If you should stop short, your dog can be thrown and injured. If the dog starts climbing on you and pestering you whilst you are driving, you will not be able to concentrate on the road. It is an unsafe situation for everyone—human and canine.

The best way to accustom your puppy to travelling in the car is by doing it gradually. Start with putting the puppy in the crate, whilst you sit behind the steering wheel. Talk to him and tell him how much he will enjoy this. Repeat this the next day and start the car, let the engine run for a couple of minutes. The day after that drive around the block and gradually extend your trips. Drive to the park and let him have a quick run and feed him when you come home. Whatever you do, make it fun for him.

Travel Tip

Never leave your dog alone in the car. In hot weather your dog can die from the high temperature inside a closed vehicle; even a car parked in the shade can heat up very quickly. Leaving the window open is dangerous as well since the dog can hurt himself trying to get out.

Travel Tip

When travelling, never let your dog off-lead in a strange area. Your dog could run away out of fear or decide to chase a passing chipmunk or cat or simply want to stretch his legs without restriction—you might never see your canine friend again.

The most acceptable, safest way of travelling with your English Springer Spaniel in a car is in a crate. It is dangerous for the dog to have free access to all parts of the vehicle whilst it is moving.

For long trips, be prepared to stop to let the dog relieve himself. Bring along whatever you need to clean up after him. You should bring along some old towels and rags, should he have an accident in the car or despite your preparations become carsick.

AIR TRAVEL
Whilst it is possible to take a dog on a flight within Britain, this is fairly unusual and advance permission is always required. The dog will be required to travel in a fibreglass crate and you should always check in advance with the airline regarding specific requirements. To help the dog be at ease, put one of his favourite toys in the crate with him. Do not feed the dog for at least six hours before the trip to minimise his need to relieve himself. However, certain regulations specify that water must always be made available to the dog in the crate.

Make sure your dog is properly identified and that your contact information appears on his ID tags and on his crate. Animals travel in a different area of the plane than human passengers so every rule must be strictly adhered to so as to prevent the risk of getting separated from your dog.

BOARDING
So you want to take a family holiday—and you want to include all members of your family. You would probably make arrangements for accommodation ahead of time anyway, but this is especially important when travelling with a dog. You do not want to make an overnight stop at the

Travel Tip

If you are going on a long motor trip with your dog, be sure the hotels are dog friendly. Many hotels do not accept dogs. Also take along some ice that can be thawed and offered to your dog if he becomes overheated. Most dogs like to lick ice.

only place around for miles to find out that they do not allow dogs. Also, you do not want to reserve a place for your family without mentioning that you are bringing a dog, because if it is against their policy you may not have a place to stay.

Alternatively, if you are travelling and choose not to bring your Springer, you will have to make arrangements for him whilst you are away. Some options are to bring him to a neighbour's house to stay whilst you are away, to have a trusted neighbour stop by often or stay at your house, or bring your dog to a reputable boarding kennel. If you choose to board him at a kennel, you should stop by to see the facility and where the dogs are kept to make sure that it is clean. Talk to the owner or the manager and see how he or she treats the dogs—do they spend time with the dogs, play with them, exercise them, etc.? You know that your Springer will not be happy unless he gets

Lost Dog?

You have a valuable dog. If the dog is lost or stolen, you would undoubtedly become extremely upset. If you encounter a lost dog, notify the police or the local animal shelter.

regular activity. Also find out the kennel's policy on vaccinations and what they require. This is for all of the dogs' safety, since when dogs are kept together, there is a greater risk of diseases being passed from dog to dog.

IDENTIFICATION

Your Springer is your valued companion and friend. That is why you always keep a close eye on him and you have made sure that he cannot escape from the garden or wriggle out of his collar and run away from you. However, accidents can happen and there

Travel Tip

The most extensive travel you do with your dog may be limited to trips to the veterinary surgeon's office—or you may decide to bring him along for long distances when the family goes on holiday. Which ever the case, it is important to consider your dog's safety while travelling.

Beware...

You should be careful where you exercise your dog. Many countryside areas have been sprayed with chemicals that are highly toxic to both dogs and humans. Never allow your dog to eat grass or drink from puddles on either public or private grounds, as the run-off water may contain chemicals from sprays and herbicides.

Did You Know?

As puppies become more and more expensive, especially those puppies of high quality for showing and/or breeding, they have a greater chance of being stolen. The usual collar dog tag is, of course, easily removed. But there are two techniques that have become widely utilised for identification.

The puppy microchip implantation involves the injection of a small microchip, about the size of a corn kernel, under the skin of the dog. If your dog shows up at a clinic or shelter, or is offered for resale under less than savory circumstances, it can be positively identified by the microchip. The microchip is scanned and a registry quickly identifies you as the owner. This is not only protection against theft, but should the dog run away or go chasing a squirrel and get lost, you have a fair chance of getting it back.

Tattooing is done on various parts of the dog, from its belly to its cheeks. The number tattooed can be your telephone number or any other number which you can easily memorise. When professional dog thieves see a tattooed dog, they usually lose interest in it. Both microchipping and tattooing can be done at your local veterinary clinic. For the safety of our dogs, no laboratory facility or dog broker will accept a tattooed dog as stock.

Tattooing for identification. This Springer has his ID number tattooed clearly across his belly.

may come a time when your dog unexpectedly gets separated from you. If this unfortunate event should occur, the first thing on your mind will be finding him. Proper identification will increase the chances of his being returned to you safely and quickly. In many countries tattooing or microchipping the puppies before they leave the breeder is common practice. This is often done by the Kennel Club so that the number that is given to the puppy either as an earmark or via the microchip is unique and can also be recorded on his pedigree.

ID tags are a traditional way of identifying your dog. Your Springer should have his tags securely fastened to his collar, which should be worn at all times.

Living with an untrained dog is a lot like owning a piano that you do not know how to play—it is a nice object to look at but it does not do much more than that to bring you pleasure. Now try taking piano lessons and suddenly the piano comes alive and brings forth magical sounds and rhythms that set your heart singing and your body swaying.

The same is true with your English Springer Spaniel. Any dog is a big responsibility and if not trained sensibly may develop unacceptable behaviour that annoys you or could even cause family friction.

To train your Springer, you may like to enrol in an obedience class. Teach him good manners as you learn how and why he

behaves the way he does. Find out how to communicate with your dog and how to recognise and understand his communications with you. Suddenly the dog takes on a new role in your life—he is clever, interesting, well behaved and fun to be with. He demonstrates his bond of devotion to you daily. In other words, your English Springer Spaniel does wonders for your ego because he constantly reminds you that you are not only his leader, you are his hero!

Those involved with teaching dog obedience and counselling owners about their dogs' behaviour have discovered some interesting facts about dog ownership. For example, training dogs when they are puppies results in the highest rate of success in developing well-mannered and well-adjusted adult dogs. Training an older dog, from six months to six years of age, can produce almost equal results providing that the owner accepts the dog's slower rate of learning capability and is willing to work patiently to help the dog succeed at developing to his fullest potential. Unfortunately, many owners of untrained adult dogs lack the patience fac-

Did You Know?

Dogs are the most honourable animals in existence. They consider another species (humans) as their own. They interface with you. You are their leader. Puppies perceive children to be on their level; their actions around small children are different than their behaviour around their adult masters.

close. He will usually follow you from room to room, will not let you out of his sight when you are outdoors with him, and respond in like manner to the people and animals you encounter. If you greet a friend warmly, he will be happy to greet the person as well. If, however, you are hesitant, even anxious, about the approach of a stranger, he will respond accordingly.

Once the puppy begins to produce hormones, his natural curiosity emerges and he begins to investigate the world around him. It is at this time when you may notice that the untrained dog begins to wander away from you and even ignore your commands to stay close.

There are usually classes within a reasonable distance of the owner's home, but you also do a lot to train your dog yourself. Sometimes there are classes available but the tuition is too costly.

All members of the family should take part in training the puppy. Your Springer should grow up to obey commands no matter who issues them.

tor, so they do not persist until their dogs are successful at learning particular behaviours.

Training a puppy, aged 10 to 16 weeks (20 weeks at the most), is like working with a dry sponge in a pool of water. The pup soaks up whatever you show him and constantly looks for more things to do and learn. At this early age, his body is not yet producing hormones, and therein lies the reason for such a high rate of success. Without hormones, he is focused on his owners and not particularly interested in investigating other places, dogs, people, etc. You are his leader: his provider of food, water, shelter and security. He latches onto you and wants to stay

Think Before You Bark!

Dogs are sensitive to their master's moods and emotions. Use your voice wisely when communicating with your dog. Never raise your voice at your dog unless you are angry and trying to correct him. 'Barking' at your dog can become as meaningless as 'dogspeak' is to you. Think before you bark!

Whatever the circumstances, the solution to the problem of lack of lesson availability lies within the pages of this book.

This chapter is devoted to helping you train your English Springer Spaniel at home. If the recommended procedures are followed faithfully, you may expect positive results that will prove rewarding to both you and your dog.

Whether your new charge is a puppy or a mature adult, the methods of teaching and the techniques we use in training basic behaviours are the same. After all, no dog, whether puppy or adult, likes harsh or inhumane methods. All creatures, however, respond favourably to gentle motivational methods and sincere praise and encouragement. Now let us get started.

Training Tip

Training a dog is a life experience. Many parents admit that much of what they know about raising children they learned from caring for their dogs. Dogs respond to love, fairness and guidance, just as children do. Become a good dog owner and you may become an even better parent.

HOUSEBREAKING

You can train a puppy to relieve itself wherever you choose, but this must be somewhere suitable. You should bear in mind from the outset that when your puppy is old enough to go out in public places, any canine deposits must be removed at once. You will always have to carry with you a small plastic bag or 'poop-scoop.'

Outdoor training includes such surfaces as grass, soil and cement. Indoor training usually means training your dog to newspaper.

When deciding on the surface and location that you will want your English Springer Spaniel to use, be sure it is going to be permanent. Training your dog to grass and then changing your mind two months later is extremely difficult for both dog and owner.

Next, choose the command you will use each and every time you want your puppy to void. 'Hurry up' and 'Toilet' are examples of commands commonly used by dog owners.

Get in the habit of giving the puppy your chosen relief command before you take him out. That way, when he becomes an adult, you will be able to determine if he wants to go out when you ask him. A confirmation will be signs of interest, wagging his tail, watching you intently, going to the door, etc.

PUPPY'S NEEDS

Puppy needs to relieve himself after play periods, after each meal, after he has been sleeping and any time he indicates that he is looking for a place to urinate or defecate.

The urinary and intestinal tract muscles of very young puppies are not fully developed. Therefore, like human babies, puppies need to relieve themselves frequently.

Take your puppy out often—every hour for an eight-week-old, for example, and always immediately after sleeping and eating. The older the puppy, the less often he will need to relieve himself. Finally, as a mature healthy adult, he will require only three to five relief trips per day.

HOUSING

Since the types of housing and control you provide for your

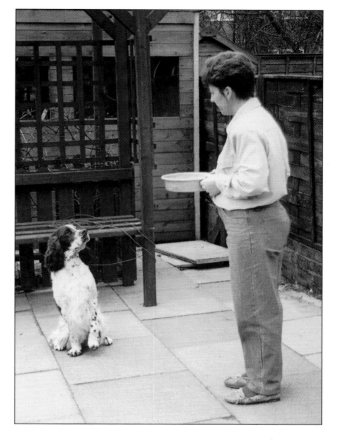

How Many Times A Day?

AGE	RELIEF TRIPS
To 14 weeks	10
14–22 weeks	8
22–32 weeks	6
Adulthood	4
(dog stops growing)	

These are estimates, of course, but they are a guide to the MINIMUM opportunities a dog should have each day to relieve itself.

puppy have a direct relationship on the success of house-training, we consider the various aspects of both before we begin training.

Bringing a new puppy home and turning him loose in your house can be compared to turning a child loose in a sports arena and telling the child that the place is all his! The sheer enormity of the place would be too much for him to handle.

Making your Springer SIT politely before he is fed reinforces that you are the one who is in charge.

85

Instead, offer the puppy clearly defined areas where he can play, sleep, eat and live. A room of the house where the family gathers is the most obvious choice. Puppies are social animals and need to feel a part of the pack right from the start. Hearing your voice, watching you whilst you are doing things and smelling you nearby are all positive reinforcers that he is now a member of your pack. Usually a family room, the kitchen or a nearby adjoining breakfast area is ideal for providing safety and security for both puppy and owner.

Within that room there should be a smaller area which the puppy can call his own. An alcove, a wire or fibreglass dog crate or a fenced (not boarded!) corner from which he can view the activities of his new family will be fine. The size of the area or crate is the key factor here. The area must be large enough for the puppy to lie down

Did You Know?

If you want to be successful in training your dog, you have four rules to obey yourself:
1. Develop an understanding of how a dog thinks.
2. Do not blame the dog for lack of communication.
3. Define your dog's personality and act accordingly.
4. Have patience and be consistent.

Did You Know?

Dogs are as different from each other as people are. What works for one dog may not work for another. Have an open mind. If one method of training is unsuccessful, try another.

and stretch out as well as stand up without rubbing his head on the top, yet small enough so that he cannot relieve himself at one end and sleep at the other without coming into contact with his droppings until fully trained to relieve himself outside.

Dogs are, by nature, clean animals and will not remain close to their relief areas unless forced to do so. In those cases, they then become dirty dogs and usually remain that way for life.

The designated area should be lined with clean bedding and a toy. Water must always be available to your puppy, though it is inadvisable to provide water whilst the pup is crated. This will only make housebreaking that much more difficult for the puppy and you.

CONTROL

By control, we mean helping the puppy to create a lifestyle pattern that will be compatible to that of his human pack (YOU!). Just as we guide little children to learn

THE SUCCESS METHOD
6 Steps to Successful Crate Training

1 Tell the puppy 'Crate time!' and place him in the crate with a small treat (a piece of cheese or half of a biscuit). Let him stay in the crate for five minutes while you are in the same room. Then release him and praise lavishly. Never release him when he is fussing. Wait until he is quiet before you let him out.

2 Repeat Step 1 several times a day.

3 The next day, place the puppy in the crate as before. Let him stay there for ten minutes. Do this several times.

4 Continue building time in five-minute increments until the puppy stays in his crate for 30 minutes with you in the room. Always take him to his relief area after prolonged periods in his crate.

5 Now go back to Step 1 and let the puppy stay in his crate for five minutes, this time while you are out of the room.

6 Once again, build crate time in five-minute increments with you out of the room. When the puppy will stay willingly in his crate (he may even fall asleep!) for 30 minutes with you out of the room, he will be ready to stay in it for several hours at a time.

our way of life, we must show the puppy when it is time to play, eat, sleep, exercise and even entertain himself.

Your puppy should always sleep in his crate. He should also learn that, during times of household confusion and excessive human activity such as at breakfast when family members are preparing for the day, he can play by himself in relative safety and comfort in his designated area. Each time you leave the puppy alone, he should understand exactly where he is to stay. You can gradually increase the time he is left alone to get him used to it.

Puppies are chewers. They cannot tell the difference

Did You Know?

Dogs will do anything for your attention. If you reward the dog when he is calm and resting, you will develop a well-mannered dog. If, on the other hand, you greet your dog excitedly and encourage him to wrestle and roughhouse with you, the dog will greet you the same way and you will have a hyper dog on your hands.

between dog bones, lamp cords, television wires, shoes, table legs, etc. Chewing into a television wire, for example, can be fatal to the puppy whilst a shorted wire can start a fire in the house. The crate keeps the pup safe and out of trouble.

If the puppy chews on the arm of the chair when he is alone, you will probably discipline him angrily when you get home. Thus, he makes the association that your coming home means he is going to be punished. (He will not remember chewing up the chair and is incapable of making the association of the discipline with his naughty deed.)

Other times of excitement, such as family parties, etc., can be fun for the puppy providing he can view the activities from the security of his crate or designated area. He is not underfoot and he is not being fed all sorts of titbits that will probably cause

Did You Know?

To a dog's way of thinking, your hands are like his mouth in terms of a defence mechanism. If you squeeze him too tightly, he might just bite you because that would be his normal response. This is not aggressive biting and, although all biting should be discouraged, you need the discipline in learning how to handle your dog.

him stomach distress, yet he still feels a part of the fun.

SCHEDULE

A puppy should be taken to his relief area each time he is released from his designated area, after meals, after a play session, when he first awakens in the morning (at age eight weeks, this can mean 5 a.m.). The puppy will indicate that he's ready 'to go' by circling or sniffing busily—do not misinterpret these signs. For a puppy less than ten weeks of age, a routine of taking him out every hour is necessary. As the puppy grows, he will be able to wait for longer periods of time.

Keep trips to his relief area short. Stay no more than five or six minutes and then return to the house. If he goes during that time, praise him lavishly and take him indoors immediately. If he does not, but he has an accident when

The Golden Rule

The golden rule of dog training is simple. For each 'question' (command), there is only one correct answer (reaction). One command = one reaction. Keep practising the command until the dog reacts correctly without hesitating. Be repetitive but not monotonous. Dogs get bored just as people do!

Canine Development Schedule

It is important to understand how and at what age a puppy develops into adulthood. If you are a puppy owner, consult the following Canine Development Schedule to determine the stage of development your puppy is currently experiencing. This knowledge will help you as you work with the puppy in the weeks and months ahead.

Period	Age	Characteristics
FIRST TO THIRD	BIRTH TO SEVEN WEEKS	Puppy needs food, sleep and warmth, and responds to simple and gentle touching. Needs mother for security and disciplining. Needs littermates for learning and interacting with other dogs. Pup learns to function within a pack and learns pack order of dominance. Begin socialising with adults and children for short periods. Begins to become aware of its environment.
FOURTH	EIGHT TO TWELVE WEEKS	Brain is fully developed. Needs socialising with outside world. Remove from mother and littermates. Needs to change from canine pack to human pack. Human dominance necessary. Fear period occurs between 8 and 16 weeks. Avoid fright and pain.
FIFTH	THIRTEEN TO SIXTEEN WEEKS	Training and formal obedience should begin. Less association with other dogs, more with people, places, situations. Period will pass easily if you remember this is pup's change-to-adolescence time. Be firm and fair. Flight instinct prominent. Permissiveness and over-disciplining can do permanent damage. Praise for good behaviour.
JUVENILE	FOUR TO EIGHT MONTHS	Another fear period about 7 to 8 months of age. It passes quickly, but be cautious of fright and pain. Sexual maturity reached. Dominant traits established. Dog should understand sit, down, come and stay by now.

NOTE: THESE ARE APPROXIMATE TIME FRAMES. ALLOW FOR INDIVIDUAL DIFFERENCES IN PUPPIES.

you go back indoors, pick him up immediately, say 'No! No!' and return to his relief area. Wait a few minutes, then return to the house again. Never hit a puppy or rub his face in urine or excrement when he has an accident! Such negativity solves nothing.

Once indoors, put the puppy in his crate until you have had time to clean up his accident. Then release him to the family area and watch him more closely than before. Chances are, his accident was a result of your not picking up his signal or waiting too long before offering him the opportunity to relieve himself. Never hold a grudge against the puppy for accidents. He will sense your resentment.

Let the puppy learn that going outdoors means it is time to

Housebreaking Tip

Do not carry your dog to his toilet area. Lead him there on a leash or, better yet, encourage him to follow you to the spot. If you start carrying him to his spot, you might end up doing this routine forever and your dog will have the satisfaction of having trained YOU.

Housebreaking Tip

Most of all, be consistent. Always take your dog to the same location, always use the same command, and always have him on lead when he is in his relief area, unless a fenced-in garden is available.

By following the Success Method, your puppy will be completely housetrained by the time his muscle and brain development reach maturity. Keep in mind that small breeds usually mature faster than large breeds, but all puppies should be trained by six months of age.

relieve himself, not play. Once trained, he will be able to play indoors and out and still differentiate between the times for play versus the times for relief.

Help him develop regular hours for naps, being alone, playing by himself and just resting, all in his crate. Encourage him to entertain himself whilst you are busy with your activities. Let him learn that having you near is comforting, but it is not your main purpose in life to provide him with undivided attention.

Each time you put a puppy in his own area, use the same command, whatever suits best. Soon, he will run to his crate or special area when he hears you say those words.

Crate training provides safety for you, the puppy and the home. It also provides the puppy with a feeling of security, and that helps the puppy achieve self-confidence and clean habits.

Remember that one of the primary ingredients in housetraining your puppy is control. Regardless of your lifestyle, there will always be occasions when you will need to have a place where your dog can stay and be happy and safe. Training is the answer for now and in the future.

In conclusion, a few key elements are really all you need for a successful house training method—consistency, frequency, praise, control and supervision. By following these procedures with a normal, healthy puppy, you and the puppy will soon be past the stage of 'accidents' and ready to move on to a full and rewarding life together.

ROLES OF DISCIPLINE, REWARD AND PUNISHMENT

Discipline, training one to act in

Once your Springer is used to his crate in the home, it will be easier to crate him for travel or other times when necessary.

accordance with rules, brings order to life. It is as simple as that. Without discipline, particularly in a group society, chaos reigns supreme and the group will eventually perish. Humans and canines are social animals and need some form of discipline in order to function effectively. They must procure food, protect their home base and their young and reproduce to keep the species going.

If there were no discipline in the lives of social animals, they would eventually die from starvation and/or predation by other stronger animals.

In the case of domestic canines, dogs need discipline in their lives in order to understand how their pack (you and other family members) functions and how they must act in order to survive.

> ## Did You Know?
>
> By providing sleeping and resting quarters that fit the dog, and offering frequent opportunities to relieve himself outside his quarters, the puppy quickly learns that the outdoors (or the newspaper if you are training him to paper) is the place to go when he needs to urinate or defecate. It also reinforces his innate desire to keep his sleeping quarters clean. This, in turn, helps develop the muscle control that will eventually produce a dog with clean living habits.

91

A wire crate offers many advantages for use in the home. Springers like to be part of the action, and wire crates offer dogs a complete view of what's going on around them.

A large humane society in a highly populated area recently surveyed dog owners regarding their satisfaction with their relationships with their dogs. People who had trained their dogs were 75% more satisfied with their pets than those who had never trained their dogs.

Dr Edward Thorndike, a psychologist, established *Thorndike's Theory of Learning*, which states that a behaviour that results in a pleasant event tends to be repeated. A behaviour that results in an unpleasant event tends not to be repeated. It is this theory on which training methods are based today. For example, if you manipulate a dog to perform a specific behaviour and reward him for doing it, he is likely to do it again because he enjoyed the end result.

Occasionally, punishment, a penalty inflicted for an offence, is necessary. The best type of punishment often comes from an outside source. For example, a child is told not to touch the stove because he may get burned. He disobeys and touches the stove. In doing so, he receives a burn. From

Be an ideal dog owner: clean up after your dog, whether it's in your own garden or a public place.

that time on, he respects the heat of the stove and avoids contact with it. Therefore, a behaviour that results in an unpleasant event tends not to be repeated.

A good example of a dog learning the hard way is the dog who chases the house cat. He is told many times to leave the cat alone, yet he persists in teasing the cat. Then, one day he begins chasing the cat but the cat turns and swipes its claws across the dog's face, leaving him with a painful gash on his nose. The final result is that the dog stops chasing the cat.

TRAINING EQUIPMENT
COLLAR AND LEAD
For an English Springer Spaniel, the collar and lead that you use for training must be one with which you are easily able to work, not too heavy for the dog and perfectly safe. Most owners opt for the lightweight nylon type, which are durable and affordable.

TREATS
Have a bag of treats on hand. Something nutritious and easy to

swallow works best. Use a soft treat, a chunk of cheese or a piece of cooked chicken rather than a dry biscuit. By the time the dog gets done chewing a dry treat, he will forget why he is being rewarded in the first place! Using food rewards will not teach a dog to beg at the table—the only way to teach a dog to beg at the table is to give him food from the table. In training, rewarding the dog with a food treat will help him associate praise and the treats with learning new behaviours that obviously please his owner.

TRAINING BEGINS: ASK THE DOG A QUESTION

In order to teach your dog any-thing, you must first get his attention. After all, he cannot learn anything if he is looking away from you with his mind on something else.

To get his attention, ask him, 'School?' and immediately walk over to him and give him a treat as you tell him, 'Good dog.' Wait a minute or two and repeat the routine, this time with a treat in your hand as you approach with-in a foot of the dog. Do not go directly to him, but stop about a foot short of him and hold out the treat as you ask, 'School?' He will see you approaching with a treat in your hand and most like-ly begin walking toward you. As you meet, give him the treat and praise again.

Your Springer will learn the rewards of proper behaviour when food treats, along with your praise, are used as motivators in training.

The third time, ask the ques-tion, have a treat in your hand and walk only a short distance toward the dog so that he must walk almost all the way to you. As he reaches you, give him the treat and praise again.

By this time, the dog will probably be getting the idea that if he pays attention to you, espe-

Training Tip

Stand up straight and authoritatively when giving your dog commands. Do not issue commands when lying on the floor or lying on your back on the sofa. If you are on your hands and knees when you give a com-mand, your dog will think you are positioning yourself to play.

93

Getting and keeping your Springer's attention are necessary before teaching something new.

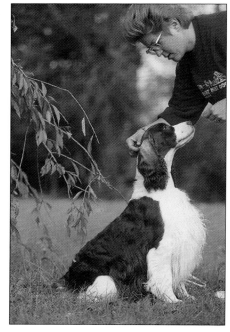

Getting and keeping your Springer's attention are necessary before teaching something new.

cially when you ask that question, it will pay off in treats and fun activities for him. In other words, he learns that 'school' means doing fun things with you that result in treats and positive attention for him.

Did You Know?

If you have other pets in the home and/or interact often with the pets of friends and other family members, your pup will respond to those pets in much the same manner as you do. It is only when you show fear or resentment toward another animal that he will act fearful or unfriendly.

Remember that the dog does not understand your verbal language, he only recognises sounds. Your question translates to a series of sounds for him, and those sounds become the signal to go to you and pay attention; if he does, he will get to interact with you plus receive treats and praise.

THE BASIC COMMANDS
TEACHING SIT

Now that you have the dog's attention, attach his lead and hold it in your left hand and a food treat in your right. Place your food hand at the dog's nose and let him lick the treat but do not let him take it from you. Say 'Sit' and slowly raise your food hand from in front of the dog's nose up over his head so that he is looking at the ceiling. As he bends his head upward, he will have to bend his knees to maintain his balance. As he bends his knees, he will assume a sit position. At that point, release the food treat and praise lavishly with comments such as 'Good dog! Good sit!', etc. Remember to always praise enthusiastically, because dogs relish verbal praise from their owners and feel so proud of themselves whenever they accomplish a good behaviour.

You will not use food forever in getting the dog to obey your commands. Food is only used to teach new behaviours, and once the dog knows what you want when you give a specific command, you will wean him off the food treats but still offer the verbal praise. After all, you will always have your voice with you, and there will be many times when you have no food rewards but expect the dog to obey.

TEACHING DOWN

Teaching the down exercise is easy when you understand how the dog perceives the down position, but it is very difficult when you do not. Dogs perceive the down position as a submissive one, therefore teaching the down exercise using a forceful method can sometimes make the dog develop such a fear of the down that he either runs away when you say 'Down' or he attempts to snap at the person who tries to force him down.

> ## Did You Know?
>
> Dogs do not understand our language. They can be trained to react to a certain sound, at a certain volume. If you say 'No, Oliver' in a very soft pleasant voice it will not have the same meaning as 'No, Oliver!!' when you shout it as loud as you can. You should never use the dog's name during a reprimand, just the command NO!! Since dogs don't understand words, comics use dogs trained with opposite meanings. Thus, when the comic commands his dog to SIT the dog will stand up; and vice versa.

Have the dog sit close alongside your left leg, facing in the same direction as you are. Hold the lead in your left hand and a food treat in your right. Now place your left hand lightly on the top of the dog's shoulders where they meet above the spinal cord. Do not push down on the dog's shoulders; simply

SIT is one of the first and most basic commands you will teach your Springer.

rest your left hand there so you can guide the dog to lie down close to your left leg rather than to swing away from your side when he drops.

Now place the food hand at the dog's nose, say 'Down' very softly (almost a whisper), and slowly lower the food hand to the dog's front feet. When the food hand reaches the floor, begin moving it forward along the floor in front of the dog. Keep talking softly to the dog, saying things like, 'Do you want this treat? You can do this, good dog.' Your reassuring tone of

Did You Know?

A dog in jeopardy never lies down. He stays alert on his feet because instinct tells him that he may have to run away or fight for his survival. Therefore, if a dog feels threatened or anxious, he will not lie down. Consequently, it is important to have the dog calm and relaxed as he learns the down exercise.

voice will help calm the dog as he tries to follow the food hand in order to get the treat.

When the dog's elbows touch the floor, release the food and praise softly. Try to get the dog to maintain that down position for several seconds before you let him sit up again. The goal here is to get the dog to settle

down and not feel threatened in the down position.

TEACHING STAY

It is easy to teach the dog to stay in either a sit or a down position. Again, we use food and praise during the teaching process as we help the dog to understand exactly what it is that we are expecting him to do.

To teach the sit/stay, start with the dog sitting on your left side as before and hold the lead in your left hand. Have a food treat in your right hand and place your food hand at the dog's nose. Say 'Stay' and step out on your right foot to stand directly in front of the dog, toe to toe, as he licks and nibbles the treat. Be sure to keep his head facing upward to maintain the sit position. Count to five and then swing around to stand next to the dog again with him on your left. As soon as you get back to the original position, release the food and praise lavishly.

To teach the down/stay, do the down as previously described. As soon as the dog lies down, say 'Stay' and step out on your right

Training Tip

Your dog is actually training you at the same time you are training him. Dogs do things to get attention. They usually repeat whatever succeeds in getting your attention.

foot just as you did in the sit/stay. Count to five and then return to stand beside the dog with him on your left side. Release the treat and praise as always.

get that treat as soon as you return to his side.

When you can stand 1 metre away from your dog for 30 seconds, you can then begin building

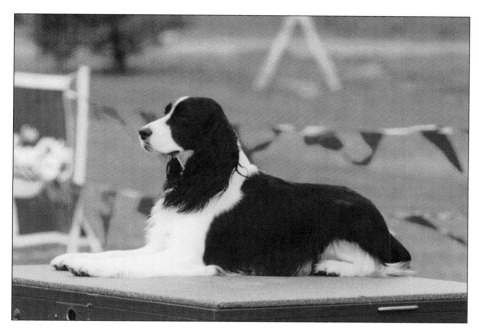

This Springer demonstrates his knowledge of the 'down/stay' command in an agility trial.

Within a week or ten days, you can begin to add a bit of distance between you and your dog when you leave him. When you do, use your left hand open with the palm facing the dog as a stay signal, much the same as the hand signal a police officer uses to stop traffic at an intersection. Hold the food treat in your right hand as before, but this time the food is not touching the dog's nose. He will watch the food hand and quickly learn that he is going to

time and distance in both stays. Eventually, the dog can be expected to remain in the stay position for prolonged periods of time until you return to him or call him to you. Always praise lavishly when he stays.

TEACHING COME
If you make teaching 'come' a fun experience, you should never have a 'student' that does not love the game or that fails to come when called. The secret, it

seems, is never to teach the word 'come.'

At times when an owner most wants his dog to come when called, the owner is likely upset or anxious and he allows these feelings to come through in the tone of his voice when he calls his dog. Hearing that desperation in his owner's voice, the dog fears the results of going to him and therefore either disobeys outright or runs in the opposite direction. The secret, therefore, is to teach the dog a game and, when you want him to come to you, simply play the game. It is practically a no-fail solution!

To begin, have several members of your family take a few food treats and each go into a different room in the house. Take turns calling the dog, and each person should celebrate the dog's finding him with a treat and lots of happy praise. When a person calls the dog, he is actually inviting the dog to find him and get a treat as a reward for 'winning.'

A few turns of the 'Where are you?' game and the dog will figure out that everyone is playing the game and that each person has a big celebration awaiting his success at locating them. Once he learns to love the game, simply calling out 'Where are you?' will bring him running from wherever he is when he hears that all-important question.

The come command is recognised as one of the most important things to teach a dog, but there are trainers who work with thousands of dogs and never teach the actual word 'Come.' Yet these dogs will race to respond to a person who uses the dog's name followed by 'Where are you?' For example, a woman has a 12-year-old companion dog who went blind, but who never fails to locate her owner when asked, 'Where are you?'

Children particularly love to play this game with their dogs. Children can hide in smaller places like a shower or bathtub, behind a bed or under a table. The dog needs to work a little bit harder to find these hiding places, but when he does he loves to celebrate

Practice Makes Perfect!

• Have training lessons with your dog every day in several short segments—three to five times a day for a few minutes at a time is ideal.

• Do not have long practice sessions. The dog will become easily bored.

• Never practice when you are tired, ill, worried or in an otherwise negative mood. This will transmit to the dog and may have an adverse effect on its performance.

Think fun, short and above all POSITIVE! End each session on a high note, rather than a failed exercise, and make sure to give a lot of praise. Enjoy the training and help your dog enjoy it, too.

with a treat and a tussle with a favourite youngster.

Training Tip

Never call your dog to come to you for a correction or scold him when he reaches you. That is the quickest way to turn a 'Come' command into 'Go away fast!' Dogs think only in the present tense, and your dog will connect the scolding with coming to you, not with the misbehaviour of a few moments earlier.

TEACHING HEEL

Heeling means that the dog walks beside the owner without pulling. It takes time and patience on the owner's part to succeed at teaching the dog that he (the owner) will not proceed unless the dog is walking calmly beside him. Pulling out ahead on the lead is definitely not acceptable.

Begin with holding the lead in your left hand as the dog sits beside your left leg. Move the loop end of the lead to your right hand but keep your left hand short on the lead so it keeps the dog in close next to you.

Say 'Heel' and step forward on your left foot. Keep the dog close to you and take three steps. Stop and have the dog sit next to you in what we now call the 'heel position.' Praise verbally, but do not touch the dog. Hesitate a moment and begin again with 'Heel,' taking three steps and stopping, at which point the dog is told to sit again.

Your goal here is to have the dog walk those three steps without pulling on the lead. When he will walk calmly beside you for three steps without pulling, increase the number of steps you take to five. When he will walk politely beside you whilst you take five steps, you can increase the length of your walk to ten steps. Keep increasing the length of your stroll until the dog will walk quietly beside you without pulling as long as you want him to heel. When you stop heeling, indicate to the dog that the exercise is over by verbally praising as you pet him and say 'OK, good dog.' The 'OK' is used as a release word meaning that the exercise is finished and the dog is free to relax.

Training Tip

When calling the dog, do not say 'Come.' Say things like, 'Rover, where are you? See if you can find me! I have a cookie for you!' Keep up a constant line of chatter with coaxing sounds and frequent questions such as, 'Where are you?' The dog will learn to follow the sound of your voice to locate you and receive his reward.

Whether gaiting in the show ring or just going for a walk around the neighbourhood, HEEL is a necessary command for every well-behaved dog.

Training Tip

If you are walking your dog and he suddenly stops and looks straight into your eyes, ignore him. Pull the leash and lead him into the direction you want to walk.

If you are dealing with a dog who insists on pulling you around, simply 'put on your brakes' and stand your ground until the dog realises that the two of you are not going anywhere until he is beside you and moving at your pace, not his. It may take some time just standing there to convince the dog that you are the leader and you will be the one to decide on the direction and speed of your travel.

Each time the dog looks up at you or slows down to give a slack lead between the two of you, quietly praise him and say, 'Good heel. Good dog.' Eventually, the dog will begin to respond and within a few days he will be walking politely beside you without pulling on the lead. At first, the training sessions should be kept short and very positive; soon the dog will be able to walk nicely with you for increasingly longer distances. Remember also to give the dog free time and the opportunity to run and play when you are done with heel practice.

WEANING OFF FOOD IN TRAINING

Food is used in training new behaviours. Once the dog understands what behaviour goes with a specific command, it is time to start weaning him off the food treats. At first, give a treat after each exercise. Then, start to give a treat only after every other exercise. Mix up the times when you offer a food reward and the times when you only offer praise so that

Did You Know?

If you start with a normal, healthy dog and give him time, patience and some carefully executed lessons, you will reap the rewards of that training for the life of the dog. And what a life it will be! The two of you will find immeasurable pleasure in the companionship you have built together with love, respect and understanding. Good luck and enjoy!

the dog will never know when he is going to receive both food and praise and when he is going to receive only praise. This is called a variable ratio reward system and it proves successful because there is always the chance that the owner will produce a treat, so the dog never stops trying for that reward. No matter what, ALWAYS give verbal praise.

> ## Training Tip
>
> Teach your dog to HEEL in an enclosed area. Once you think the dog will obey reliably and you want to attempt advanced obedience exercises such as off-lead heeling, test him in a fenced in area so he cannot run away.

OBEDIENCE CLASSES

It is a good idea to enrol in an obedience class if one is available in your area. If yours is a show dog, ringcraft classes would be more appropriate. Many areas have dog clubs that offer basic obedience training as well as preparatory classes for obedience competition. There are also local dog trainers who offer similar classes.

At obedience trials, dogs can earn titles at various levels of competition. The beginning levels of competition include basic behaviours such as sit, down, heel, etc. The more advanced levels of com-

petition include jumping, retrieving, scent discrimination and signal work. The advanced levels require a dog and owner to put a lot of time and effort into their training and the titles that can be earned at these levels of competition are very prestigious.

> ## Training Tip
>
> If you begin teaching the heel by taking long walks and letting the dog pull you along, he misinterprets this action as an acceptable form of taking a walk. When you pull back on the lead to counteract his pulling, he reads that tug as a signal to pull even harder!

Once your Springer is housetrained and proficient in basic commands, the everyday routine will become second nature to him. These Springers wait politely by the door to be let back inside.

OTHER ACTIVITIES FOR LIFE

Whether a dog is trained in the structured environment of a class or alone with his owner at home, there are many activities that can bring fun and rewards to both owner and dog once they have mastered basic control.

Teaching the dog to help out around the home, in the garden or on the farm provides great satisfaction to both dog and owner. In addition, the dog's help makes life a little easier for his owner and raises his stature as a valued companion to his family. It helps give the dog a purpose by occupying his mind and providing an outlet for his energy.

Backpacking is an exciting and healthy activity that the dog can be taught without assistance from more than his owner. The exercise of walking and climbing is good for man and dog alike, and the bond that they develop together is priceless.

Springers can be trained to participate in many fun activities...although this Springer seems to have found something more interesting than his 'sled-dog' duties.

> ## Training Tip
>
> Never train your dog, puppy or adult, when you are mad or in a sour mood. Dogs are very sensitive to human feelings, especially anger, and if your dog senses that you are angry or upset, he will connect your anger with his training and learn to resent or fear his training sessions.

If you are interested in participating in organised competition with your English Springer Spaniel, there are activities other than obedience in which you and your dog can become involved. Agility is a popular and fun sport where dogs run through an obsta-

> ## The Success Method
>
> Success that comes by luck is usually short lived. Success that comes by well-thought-out proven methods is often more easily achieved and permanent. This is the Success Method. It is designed to give you, the puppy owner, a simple yet proven way to help your puppy develop clean living habits and a feeling of security in his new environment.

Obedience School

A basic obedience beginner's class usually lasts for six to eight weeks. Dog and owner attend an hour-long lesson once a week and practise for a few minutes, several times a day, each day at home. If done properly, the whole procedure will result in a well-mannered dog and an owner who delights in living with a pet that is eager to please and enjoys doing things with his owner.

cle course that includes various jumps, tunnels and other exercises to test the dog's speed and coordination. The owners run through the course beside their dogs to give commands and to guide them through the course. Although competitive, the focus is on fun—it's fun to do, fun to watch, and great exercise.

GUNDOG TRAINING

The spaniel's duties in the field consist of working close to the sportsman, to quest for game, flush it and retrieve it when called upon to do so. The Springer is the dog for the rough shooter, i.e., the man who goes out by himself in search of game, be it fur or feather.

If you want to train your Springer Spaniel for work, you have to start at an early age. The basis for every training is obedience and that is where you start

Obedience School

Taking your dog to an obedience school may be the best investment in time and money you can ever make. You will enjoy the benefits for the lifetime of your dog and you will have the opportunity to meet people with your similar expectations for companion dogs.

Training your Springer to hand signals is an advanced form of training. Start using hand signals along with verbal commands to teach your dog their meaning.

103

The English Springer Spaniel is a sporting dog by instinct and will respond to being trained for work at an early age.

with your puppy immediately. Basic commands such as 'come,' 'sit' and 'heel' can be taught to the puppy. Everything he learns when he is under six months old won't be forgotten. You can also start to teach him to retrieve a small object or dummy. This can be a sock or a rabbit skin or a wing of a bird. If you throw the object a few yards ahead of your puppy, he will run to it and pick it up. Call him by his name and encourage him to bring it back to you. Don't be discouraged if your puppy thinks this is a lovely game and runs off with the object! If he does that, move away from him, calling him by his name. Always remember to reward him whenever possible.

The next lesson is to encourage him to use his nose. By dragging a piece of tripe you can make a trail for him to work out. You can also throw the dummy into light cover, out of sight, and encourage your Springer to locate and then retrieve it. You must be very careful with the puppy when he starts teething because picking up the dummy might be quite painful and forcing him to pick it up would do irreparable harm to his willingness to retrieve. By the time your puppy is eight or nine months old, knows his basic obedience and has learned to retrieve and use his nose, you can join a training class. Depending on his natural aptitude, you can train for many different pursuits, from working and spaniel tests to tracking and more.

Springers often do well in agility trials. This Springer conquers the obstacles with ease.

Springers are trained to retrieve dummies before they are used to retrieve game. Springers are known to have 'soft mouths,' meaning that they exert minimum pressure on whatever they carry in their mouths so as not to damage it.

Did You Know?

Occasionally, a dog and owner who have not attended formal classes have been able to earn entry-level titles by obtaining competition rules and regulations from a local kennel club and practising on their own to a degree of perfection. Obtaining the higher level titles, however, almost always requires extensive training under the tutelage of experienced instructors. In addition, the more difficult levels require more specialised equipment whereas the lower levels do not.

Retrieving over a fence—a working Springer's job is to bring the game (or, in this case, the dummy) to his master, without letting anything get in his way.

105

Above: Candid photos of an actual hunt. The English Springer Spaniels are alert and ready to work.

Opposite page:
(Top) The Springer successfully returns the dummy to his master.
(Bottom) Using hand signals, the owner commands the dog to 'down/stay.'

107

Internal Organs with Skeletal Structure

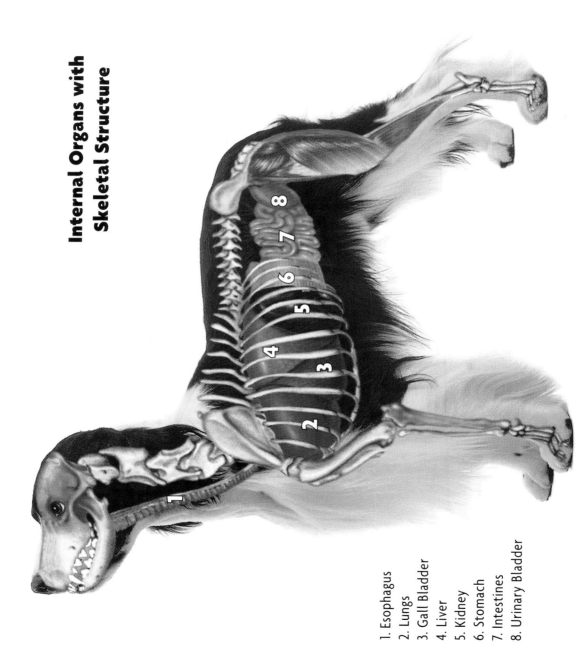

1. Esophagus
2. Lungs
3. Gall Bladder
4. Liver
5. Kidney
6. Stomach
7. Intestines
8. Urinary Bladder

Dogs suffer many of the same physical illnesses as people. Since most people know more about human diseases than canine maladies, many of the terms used in this chapter will be familiar but not necessarily those used by veterinary surgeons. We will use the term *x-ray*, instead of the more acceptable term *radiograph*. We will also use the familiar term *symptoms* even though dogs don't have symptoms, which are verbal descriptions of the patient's feelings—dogs have *clinical signs*. Since dogs can't speak, we have to look for clinical signs...but we still use the term symptoms in this book.

As a general rule, medicine is practised. That term is not arbitrary. Medicine is a constantly changing art as we learn more and more about genetics, electronic aids (like CAT scans) and daily laboratory advances. There are many dog maladies, like canine hip dysplasia, which are not universally treated in the same manner. Some veterinary surgeons opt for surgery more often than others do.

SELECTING A VETERINARY SURGEON

Your selection of a veterinary surgeon should not be based upon personality (as most are) but upon their convenience to your home. You want a vet who is close because you might have emergencies or need to make multiple visits for treatments. You want a vet who has services that you might

Before you buy your English Springer Spaniel, meet and interview the veterinary surgeons in your area. Take everything into consideration—discuss his background, specialities, fees, emergency policy, etc.

109

A typical American vet's income categorised according to services performed. This survey dealt with small-animal (pet) practices.

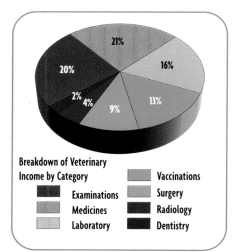

Breakdown of Veterinary Income by Category

Examinations
Medicines
Laboratory
Vaccinations
Surgery
Radiology
Dentistry

A typical American vet's income categorised according to services performed. This survey dealt with small-animal (pet) practices.

require such as grooming facilities as well as sophisticated pet supplies and a good reputation for ability and responsiveness. There is nothing more frustrating than having to wait a day or more to get a response from your veterinary surgeon.

All veterinary surgeons are licensed and their diplomas and/or certificates should be displayed in their waiting rooms. There are, however, many veterinary specialities that usually require further studies and internships. There are specialists in heart problems (veterinary cardiologists), skin problems (veterinary dermatologists), teeth and gum problems (veterinary dentists), eye problems (veterinary ophthalmologists), x-rays (veterinary radiologists), and surgeons who have specialities in bones,

muscles or other organs. Most veterinary surgeons do routine surgery such as neutering, stitching up wounds and docking tails for those breeds in which such is required for show purposes. When the problem affecting your dog is serious, it is not unusual or impudent to get another medical opinion, although in Britain you are obliged to advise the vets concerned about this. You might also want to compare costs amongst several veterinary surgeons. Sophisticated health care and veterinary services can be very costly. Don't be bashful about discussing these costs with your veterinary surgeon or his staff. It is not infrequent that important decisions are based upon financial considerations.

PREVENTATIVE MEDICINE
It is much easier, less costly and more effective to practise preventative medicine than to fight bouts of illness and disease. Properly bred puppies come from parents that were selected based upon their genetic disease profile. Their mothers should have been vaccinated, free of all internal and external parasites, and properly nourished. For these reasons, a visit to the veterinary surgeon who cared for the dam (mother) is recommended. The dam can pass on disease resistance to her puppies, which can last for eight to ten weeks. She can also pass on

First Aid at a Glance

Burns
Place the affected area under cool water; use ice if only a small area is burnt.

Bee/Insect bites
Apply ice to relieve swelling; antihistamine dosed properly.

Animal bites
Clean any bleeding area; apply pressure until bleeding subsides; go to the vet.

Spider bites
Use cold compress and a pressurised pack to inhibit venom's spreading.

Antifreeze poisoning
Immediately induce vomiting by using hydrogen peroxide.

Fish hooks
Removal best handled by vet; hook must be cut in order to remove.

Snake bites
Pack ice around bite; contact vet quickly; identify snake for proper antivenin.

Car accident
Move dog from roadway with blanket; seek veterinary aid.

Shock
Calm the dog, keep him warm; seek immediate veterinary help.

Nosebleed
Apply cold compress to the nose; apply pressure to any visible abrasion.

Bleeding
Apply pressure above the area; treat wound by applying a cotton pack.

Heat stroke
Submerge dog in cold bath; cool down with fresh air and water; go to the vet.

Frostbite/Hypothermia
Warm the dog with a warm bath, electric blankets or hot water bottles.

Abrasions
Clean the wound and wash out thoroughly with fresh water; apply antiseptic.

!! *Remember: an injured dog may attempt to bite a helping hand from fear and confusion. Always muzzle the dog before trying to offer assistance.* !!

HEALTH AND VACCINATION SCHEDULE

AGE IN WEEKS:	3RD	6TH	8TH	10TH	12TH	14TH	16TH	20-24TH
Worm Control	✔	✔	✔	✔	✔	✔	✔	✔
Neutering								✔
Heartworm		✔						✔
Parvovirus		✔		✔		✔		✔
Distemper			✔		✔		✔	
Hepatitis			✔		✔		✔	
Leptospirosis		✔		✔		✔		
Parainfluenza		✔		✔		✔		
Dental Examination			✔					✔
Complete Physical			✔					✔
Temperament Testing			✔					
Coronavirus					✔			
Kennel Cough		✔						
Hip Dysplasia							✔	
Rabies								✔

Vaccinations are not instantly effective. It takes about two weeks for the dog's immunisation system to develop antibodies. Most vaccinations require annual booster shots. Your veterinary surgeon should guide you in this regard.

An English Springer Spaniel getting a routine examination.

Did You Know?

Vaccines do not work all the time. Sometimes dogs are allergic to them and many times the antibodies, which are supposed to be stimulated by the vaccine, just are not produced. You should keep your dog in the veterinary clinic for an hour after it is vaccinated to be sure there are no allergic reactions.

parasites and many infections. That's why you should visit the veterinary surgeon who cared for the dam.

WEANING TO FIVE MONTHS OLD
Puppies should be weaned by the time they are about two months old. A puppy that remains for at least eight weeks with its mother and litter mates usually adapts better to other dogs and people later in its life.

Some new owners have their puppy examined by a veterinary surgeon immediately, that is a good idea. Vaccination pro-grammes usually begin when the puppy is very young.

The veterinary surgeon takes the Springer's temperature.

Disease	What is it?	What causes it?	Symptoms
Leptospirosis	Severe disease that affects the internal organs; can be spread to people.	A bacterium, which is often carried by rodents, that enters through mucous membranes and spreads quickly throughout the body.	Range from fever, vomiting and loss of appetite in less severe cases to shock, irreversible kidney damage and possibly death in most severe cases.
Rabies	Potentially deadly virus that infects warm-blooded mammals. Not seen in United Kingdom.	Bite from a carrier of the virus, mainly wild animals.	1st stage: dog exhibits change in behaviour, fear. 2nd stage: dog's behaviour becomes more aggressive. 3rd stage: loss of coordination, trouble with bodily functions.
Parvovirus	Highly contagious virus, potentially deadly.	Ingestion of the virus, which is usually spread through the faeces of infected dogs.	Most common: severe diarrhoea. Also vomiting, fatigue, lack of appetite.
Kennel cough	Contagious respiratory infection.	Combination of types of bacteria and virus. Most common: *Bordetella bronchiseptica* bacteria and parainfluenza virus.	Chronic cough.
Distemper	Disease primarily affecting respiratory and nervous system.	Virus that is related to the human measles virus.	Mild symptoms such as fever, lack of appetite and mucous secretion progress to evidence of brain damage, 'hard pad.'
Hepatitis	Virus primarily affecting the liver.	Canine adenovirus type I (CAV-1). Enters system when dog breathes in particles.	Lesser symptoms include listlessness, diarrhoea, vomiting. More severe symptoms include 'blue-eye' (clumps of virus in eye).
Coronavirus	Virus resulting in digestive problems.	Virus is spread through infected dog's faeces.	Stomach upset evidenced by lack of appetite, vomiting, diarrhoea.

The puppy will have its teeth examined and have its skeletal conformation and general health checked prior to certification by the veterinary surgeon. Puppies in certain breeds have problems with their kneecaps, eye cataracts and other eye problems, heart murmurs and undescended testicles. They may also have personality problems and your veterinary surgeon might have training in temperament evaluation.

VACCINATION SCHEDULING
Most vaccinations are given by injection and should only be done by a veterinary surgeon. Both he and you should keep a record of the date of the injection, the identification of the vaccine and the amount given. Some vets give a first vaccination at eight weeks, but most dog breeders prefer the course not to commence until about ten weeks because of negating any antibodies

Did You Know?

Your veterinary surgeon will probably recommend that your puppy be vaccinated before you take him outside. There are airborne diseases, parasite eggs in the grass and unexpected visits from other dogs that might be dangerous to your puppy's health.

Did You Know?

Cases of hyperactive adrenal glands (Cushing's disease) have been traced to the drinking of highly chlorinated water. Aerate or age your dog's drinking water before offering it.

passed on by the dam. The vaccination scheduling is usually based on a 15-day cycle. You must take your vet's advice as to when to vaccinate as this may differ according to the vaccine used. Most vaccinations immunise your puppy against viruses.

The usual vaccines contain immunising doses of several different viruses such as distemper, parvovirus, parainfluenza and hepatitis. There are other vaccines available when the puppy is at risk. You should rely upon professional advice. This is especially true for the booster-shot programme. Most vaccination programmes require a booster when the puppy is a year old and once a year thereafter. In some cases, circumstances may require more frequent immunisations.

Kennel cough, more formally known as tracheobronchitis, is treated with a vaccine that is sprayed into the dog's nostrils. Kennel cough is usually included in routine vaccination, but this is often not so effective as for other major diseases.

Normal English Springer Spaniel Skeleton

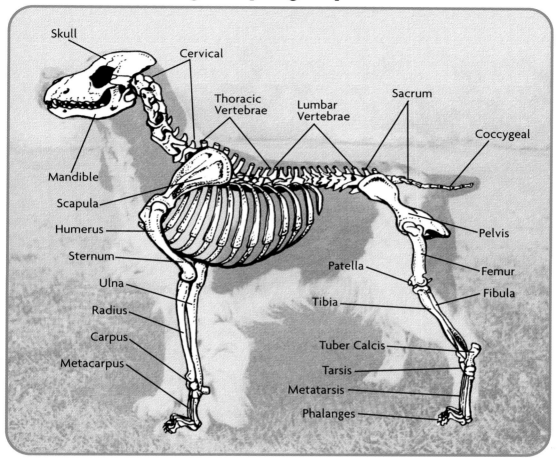

Skull · Cervical · Thoracic Vertebrae · Lumbar Vertebrae · Sacrum · Coccygeal · Mandible · Scapula · Humerus · Sternum · Ulna · Radius · Carpus · Metacarpus · Patella · Tibia · Tuber Calcis · Tarsis · Metatarsis · Phalanges · Pelvis · Femur · Fibula

FIVE MONTHS TO ONE YEAR OF AGE
Unless you intend to breed or show your dog, neutering the puppy at six months of age is recommended. Discuss this with your veterinary surgeon. Neutering has proven to be extremely beneficial to both male and female puppies. Besides eliminating the possibility of pregnancy, it inhibits (but does not prevent) breast cancer in bitches and

Did You Know?

Not every dog's ears are the same. Ears that are open to the air are healthier than ears with poor air circulation. Sometimes a dog can have two differently shaped ears. You should not probe inside your dog's ears. Only clean that which is accessible with a soft cotton wipe.

Did You Know?

A dental examination is in order when the dog is between six months and one year of age so any permanent teeth that have erupted incorrectly can be corrected. It is important to begin a brushing routine, preferably using a two-sided brushing technique, whereby both sides of the tooth are brushed at the same time. Durable nylon and safe edible chews should be a part of your puppy's arsenal for good health, good teeth and pleasant breath. The vast majority of dogs three to four years old and older has diseases of the gums from lack of dental attention. Using the various types of dental chews can be very effective in controlling dental plaque.

prostate cancer in male dogs. Under no circumstances should a bitch be spayed prior to her first season.

Dogs Older Than One Year
Continue to visit the veterinary surgeon at least once a year. There is no such disease as old age, but bodily functions do change with age. The eyes and ears are no longer as efficient. Liver, kidney and intestinal functions often decline. Proper dietary changes, recommended by your veterinary surgeon, can make life more

pleasant for the ageing English Springer Spaniel and you.

SKIN PROBLEMS IN ENGLISH SPRINGER SPANIELS
Veterinary surgeons are consulted by dog owners for skin problems more than any other group of diseases or maladies. Dogs' skin is almost as sensitive as human skin and both suffer almost the same ailments (though the occurrence of acne in dogs is rare!). For this reason, veterinary dermatology has developed into a speciality practised by many veterinary surgeons.

Since many skin problems have visual symptoms that are almost identical, it requires the skill of an experienced veterinary dermatologist to identify and cure many of the more severe skin disorders. Pet shops sell many treatments for skin problems but most of the treatments are directed at symptoms and not the underlying problem(s). If your dog is suffering from a skin disorder, you should seek professional assistance as quickly as possible. As with all diseases, the earlier a problem is identified and treated, the more successful is the cure.

Parasite Bites
Many of us are allergic to insect bites. The bites itch, erupt and may even become infected. Dogs have the same reaction to fleas, ticks and/or

mites. When an insect lands on you, you have the chance to whisk it away with your hand. Unfortunately, when our dog is bitten by a flea, tick or mite, it can only scratch it away or bite it. By the time the dog has been bitten, the parasite has done some of its damage. It may also have laid eggs to cause further problems in the near future. The itching from parasite bites is probably due to the saliva injected into the site when the parasite sucks the dog's blood.

Did You Know?

Feeding your dog properly is very important. An incorrect diet could affect the dog's health, behaviour and nervous system, possibly making a normal dog into an aggressive one.

AUTO-IMMUNE SKIN CONDITIONS

Auto-immune skin conditions are commonly referred to as being allergic to yourself, whilst allergies are usually inflammatory reactions to an outside stimulus. Auto-immune diseases cause serious damage to the tissues that are involved.

The best known auto-immune disease is lupus, which affects people as well as dogs. The symptoms are variable and may affect the kidneys, bones, blood chemistry and skin. It can be fatal to both

dogs and humans, though it is not thought to be transmissible. It is usually successfully treated with cortisone, prednisone or similar corticosteroid, but extensive use of these drugs can have harmful side effects.

AIRBORNE ALLERGIES

An interesting allergy is pollen allergy. Humans have hay fever, rose fever and other fevers with which they suffer during the pollinating season. Many dogs suffer the same allergies. When the pollen count is high, your dog might suffer but don't expect them to sneeze and have runny noses like humans. Dogs react to pollen allergies the same way they react to fleas—they scratch and bite themselves.

Dogs, like humans, can be tested for allergens. Discuss the testing with your veterinary dermatologist.

FOOD PROBLEMS
FOOD ALLERGIES

Dogs are allergic to many foods that are best sellers and highly recommended by breeders and veterinary surgeons. Changing the brand of food that you buy may not eliminate the problem if the element to which the dog is allergic is contained in the new brand.

Recognising a food allergy is difficult. Humans vomit or have rashes when they eat a food to which they are allergic. Dogs nei-

117

ther vomit nor (usually) develop a rash. They react in the same manner as they do to an airborne or flea allergy: they itch, scratch and bite. Thus making the diagnosis extremely difficult. Whilst pollen allergies and parasite bites are usually seasonal, food allergies are year-round problems.

FOOD INTOLERANCE

Food intolerance is the inability of the dog to completely digest certain foods. Puppies that may have done very well on their mother's milk may not do well on cow's milk. The result of this food intolerance may be loose bowels, passing gas and stomach pains. These are the only obvious symptoms of food intolerance and that makes diagnosis difficult.

TREATING FOOD PROBLEMS

It is possible to handle food allergies and food intolerance yourself. Put your dog on a diet that it has never had. Obviously if it has never eaten this new food, it can't have been allergic or intolerant of it. Start with a

Dogs, like humans, can be allergic to certain foods. For this reason, find a well-balanced dog food and do not vary from it. Additional supplements are not necessary unless recommended by the vet.

Did You Know?

The myth that dogs need extra fat in their diets can be harmful. Should your vet recommend extra fat, use safflower oil instead of animal oils. Safflower oil has been shown to be less likely to cause allergic reactions.

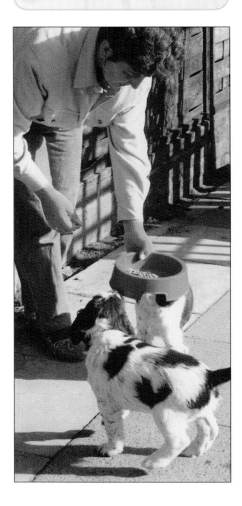

Did You Know?

Chances are that you and your dog will have the same allergies. Your allergies are readily recognisable and usually easily treated. Your dog's allergies may be masked.

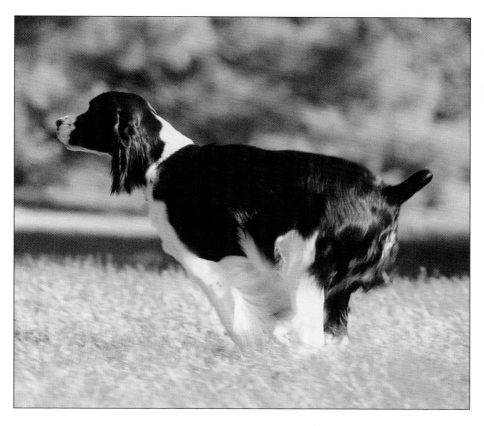

Check your Springer's stool from time to time. He should not be straining, and the stool should be well formed and with no indication of worms.

single ingredient that is not in the dog's diet at the present time, such as raw tripe and wholemeal bread. Keep the dog on this diet (with no additives) for a month. If the symptoms of food allergy or intolerance disappear, don't go back to his old diet, but stick to the tripe and bread and add one ingredient of his former diet. Let the dog stay on the modified diet for a month before you add another ingredient. It will take some time but you will find out which is the ingredient that caused the problems.

An alternative method is to carefully study the ingredients in the diet to which your dog is allergic or intolerant. Identify the main ingredient in this diet and eliminate the main ingredient by buying a different food that does not have that ingredient. Keep experimenting until the symptoms disappear after one month on the new diet.

A scanning electron micrograph (S. E. M.) of a dog flea, *Ctenocephalides canis.*

S. E. M. BY DR DENNIS KUNKEL, UNIVERSITY OF HAWAII

EXTERNAL PARASITES

Of all the problems to which dogs are prone, none is more well known and frustrating than fleas. Flea infestation, is relatively simple to cure but difficult to prevent. Parasites that are

Opposite page: A scanning electron micrograph of a dog or cat flea, *Ctenocephalides,* magnified more than 100x. This has been colourised for effect.

Magnified head of a dog flea, *Ctenocephalides canis.*

Did You Know?

Fleas have been around for millions of years and have adapted to changing host animals.

They are able to go through a complete life cycle in less than one month or they can extend their lives to almost two years by remaining as pupae or cocoons. They do not need blood or any other food for up to 20 months.

They have been measured as being able to jump 300,000 times and can jump 150 times their length in any direction including straight up. Those are just a few of the reasons they are so successful in infesting a dog!

harboured inside the body are a bit more difficult to eradicate but they are easier to control.

FLEAS

To control a flea infestation you have to understand the flea's life cycle. Fleas are often thought of as a summertime problem but centrally heated homes have changed the patterns and fleas can be found at any time of the year. The most effective method of flea control is a two-stage approach: one stage to kill the adult fleas, and the other to control the development of pre-adult fleas. Unfortunately, no single active ingredient is effective against all stages of the life cycle.

LIFE CYCLE STAGES

During its life, a flea will pass through four life stages: egg, larva, pupa and adult. The adult stage is the most visible and irritating stage of the flea life cycle

S. E. M. BY DR DENNIS KUNKEL, UNIVERSITY OF HAWAII

S. E. M. BY DR DENNIS KUNKEL, UNIVERSITY OF HAWAII

The Life Cycle of the Flea

Adult

Pupa

Larva

Egg

The life cycle of the flea was posterised by Fleabusters'. Poster courtesy of Fleabusters', R$_x$ for Fleas.

and this is why the majority of flea-control products concentrate on this stage. The fact is that adult fleas account for only 1% of the total flea population, and the other 99% exist in pre-adult stages, i.e., eggs, larvae and pupae. The pre-adult stages are barely visible to the naked eye.

PHOTO BY JEAN CLAUDE REVY/PHOTOTAKE.

THE LIFE CYCLE OF THE FLEA

Eggs are laid on the dog, usually in quantities of about 20 or 30, several times a day. The female adult flea must have a blood meal before each egg-laying session. When first laid, the eggs will cling to the dog's fur, as the eggs are still moist. However, they will quickly dry out and fall from the dog, especially if the dog moves around or scratches. Many eggs will fall off in the dog's favourite area or an area in which

On Guard: Catching Fleas Off Guard

Consider the following ways to arm yourself against fleas:

• Add a small amount of pennyroyal or eucalyptus oil to your dog's bath. These natural remedies repel fleas.

• Supplement your dog's food with fresh garlic (minced or grated) and a hearty amount of brewer's yeast, both of which ward off fleas.

• Use a flea comb on your dog daily. Submerge fleas in a cup of bleach to kill them quickly.

• Confine the dog to only a few rooms to limit the spread of fleas in the home.

• Vacuum daily...and get all of the crevices! Dispose of the bag every few days until the problem is under control.

• Wash your dog's bedding daily. Cover cushions where your dog sleeps with towels, and wash the towels often.

A male dog flea, *Ctenocephalides canis*.

PHOTO BY JEAN CLAUDE REVY/PHOTOTAKE.

The eggs of the dog flea.

Male cat fleas, *Ctenocephalides felis*, are very commonly found on dogs.

Dwight R Kuhn's magnificent action photo showing a flea jumping from a dog's back.

he spends a lot of time, such as his bed.

Once the eggs fall from the dog onto the carpet or furniture, they will hatch into larvae. This takes from one to ten days. Larvae are not particularly mobile, and will usually travel only a few inches from where they hatch. However, they do have a tendency to move away from light and heavy traffic—under furniture and behind doors are common places to find high quantities of flea larvae.

The flea larvae feed on dead organic matter, including adult flea faeces, until they are ready to change into adult fleas. Fleas will usually remain as larvae for around seven days. After this period, the larvae will pupate into protective pupae. While inside the pupae, the larvae will undergo metamorphosis and change into

PHOTO BY DWIGHT R KUHN.

adult fleas. This can take as little time as a few days, but the adult fleas can remain inside the pupae waiting to hatch for up to two years. The pupae are signalled to hatch by certain stimuli, such as physical pressure—the pupae's being stepped on, heat from an animal lying on the pupae or increased carbon dioxide levels and vibrations—indicating that a suitable host is available.

Once hatched, the adult flea must feed within a few days. Once the adult flea finds a host, it will not leave voluntarily. It only becomes dislodged by grooming or the host animal's scratching. The adult flea will remain on the host for the duration of its life unless forcibly removed.

TREATING THE ENVIRONMENT AND THE DOG

Treating fleas should be a two-pronged attack. First, the environment needs to be treated; this includes carpets and furniture,

Human lice look like dog lice; the two are closely related.

PHOTO BY DWIGHT R KUHN.

Did You Know?

Never mix flea control products without first consulting your veterinary surgeon. Some products can become toxic when combined with others and can cause serious or fatal consequences.

The second stage of treatment is to apply an adult insecticide to the dog. Traditionally, this would be in the form of a collar or a spray, but more recent innovations include digestible insecticides that poison the fleas when they ingest the dog's blood. Alternatively, there are drops that, when placed on the back of the animal's neck, spread throughout the fur and skin to kill adult fleas.

especially the dog's bedding and areas underneath furniture. The environment should be treated with a household spray containing an Insect Growth Regulator (IGR) and an insecticide to kill the adult flea. Most IGRs are effective against eggs and larvae; they actually mimic the fleas' own hormones and stop the eggs and larvae from developing into adult fleas. There are currently no treatments available to attack the pupa stage of the life cycle, so the adult insecticide is used to kill the newly hatched adult fleas before they find a host. Most IGRs are active for many months, whilst adult insecticides are only active for a few days.

When treating with a household spray, it is a good idea to vacuum before applying the product. This stimulates as many pupae as possible to hatch into adult fleas. The vacuum cleaner should also be treated with a flea treatment to prevent the eggs and larvae that have been hoovered into the vacuum bag from hatching.

Did You Know?

Two types of products should be used when treating fleas—a product to treat the pet and a product to treat the home. Adult fleas represent less than 1% of the flea population. The pre-adult fleas (eggs, larvae and pupae) represent more than 99% of the flea population and are found in the environment; it is in the case of pre-adult fleas that products containing an Insect Growth Regulator (IGR) should be used in the home.

IGRs are a new class of compounds used to prevent the development of insects. They do not kill the insect outright, but instead use the insect's biology against it to stop it from completing its growth. Products that contain methoprene are the world's first and leading IGRs. Used to control fleas and other insects, this type of IGR will stop flea larvae from developing and protect the house for up to seven months.

TICKS AND MITES

Though not as common as fleas, ticks and mites are found all over the tropical and temperate world. They don't bite, like fleas; they harpoon. They dig their sharp proboscis (nose) into the dog's skin and drink the blood. Their only food and drink is dog's blood. Dogs can get Lyme disease, Rocky Mountain spotted fever (normally found in the USA only), paralysis and many other diseases from ticks and mites. They may live where fleas are found and they like to hide in cracks or seams in walls wherever dogs live. They are controlled the same way fleas are controlled.

The dog tick, *Dermacentor variabilis*, may well be the most common dog tick in many geographical areas, especially those areas where the climate is hot and humid.

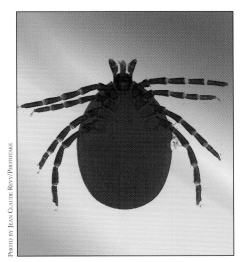

An uncommon dog tick of the genus *Ixode*. Magnified 10x.

Most dog ticks have life expectancies of a week to six months, depending upon climatic conditions. They can neither jump nor fly, but they can crawl slowly and can range up to 5 metres (16 feet) to reach a sleeping or unsuspecting dog.

MANGE

Mites cause a skin irritation called mange. Some are contagious, like *Cheyletiella*, ear mites, scabies and chiggers. The non-contagious mites are *Demodex*. Mites that cause ear-mite infestation are usually controlled with ivermectin, which is often toxic to Collies and probably should be avoided in all herding breeds.

It is essential that your dog be treated for mange as quickly as possible because some forms of mange are transmissible to people.

Opposite page: The dog tick, *Dermacentor variabilis*, is probably the most common tick found on dogs. Look at the strength in its eight legs! No wonder it's hard to detach them.

A brown dog tick, *Rhipicephalus sanguineus*, is an uncommon but annoying tick found on dogs.

127

Photo by Jean Claude Revy/Phototake.

Photo by Carolina Biological Supply/Phototake.

Two views of the mange mite, *Psoroptes bovis.*

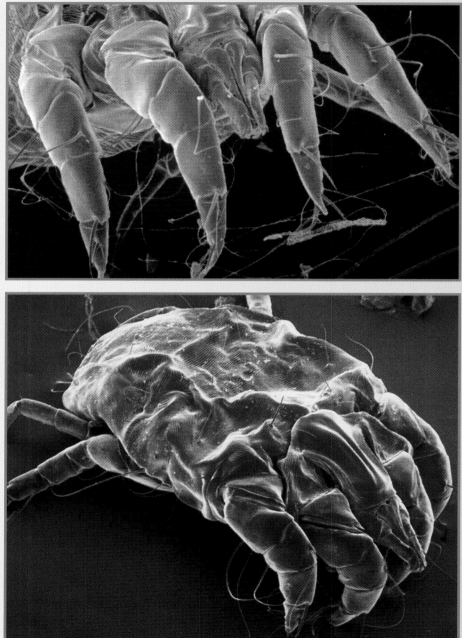

SEM by James Hayden-Yoav/Phototake

SEM by James Hayden-Yoav/Phototake

INTERNAL PARASITES

Most animals—fishes, birds and mammals, including dogs and humans—have worms and other parasites that live inside their bodies. According to Dr Herbert R Axelrod, the fish pathologist, there are two kinds of parasites: dumb and smart. The smart parasites live in peaceful cooperation with their hosts (symbiosis), while the dumb parasites kill their host. Most of the worm infections are relatively easy to control. If they are not controlled they eventually weaken the host dog to the point that other medical problems occur, but they are not dumb parasites.

ROUNDWORMS

The roundworms that infect dogs are scientifically known as *Toxocara canis*. They live in the dog's intestine. The worms shed eggs continually. It has been estimated that a dog produces about 150 grammes of faeces every day. Each gramme of faeces averages 10,000–12,000 eggs of roundworms. There are no known areas in which dogs roam that do not contain roundworm eggs. The greatest danger of roundworms

Did You Know?

Ridding your puppy of worms is VERY IMPORTANT because certain worms that puppies carry, such as tapeworms and roundworms, can infect humans.

Breeders initiate a deworming programme at or about four weeks of age. The routine is repeated every two or three weeks until the puppy is three months old. The breeder from whom you obtained your puppy should provide you with the complete details of the deworming programme.

Your veterinary surgeon can prescribe and monitor the programme of deworming for you. The usual programme is treating the puppy every 15–20 days until the puppy is positively worm free.

It is not advised that you treat your puppy with drugs that are not recommended professionally.

PHOTO BY CAROLINA BIOLOGICAL SUPPLY/PHOTOTAKE.

The roundworm, *Rhabditis*. The roundworm can infect both dogs and humans.

The roundworm *Rhabditis*.

Photo by Carolina Biological Supply/Phototake.

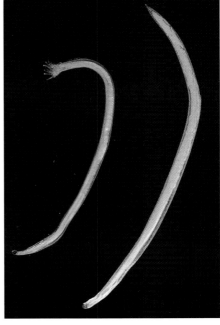

Photo by Dwight R Kuhn.

Male and female hookworms, *Ancylostoma caninum*, are uncommonly found in pet or show dogs in Britain. Hookworms may infect other dogs that have exposure to grasslands.

is that they infect people, too! It is wise to have your dog tested regularly for roundworms.

Pigs also have roundworm infections that can be passed to human and dogs. The typical roundworm parasite is called *Ascaris lumbricoides*.

HOOKWORMS

The worm *Ancylostoma caninum* is commonly called the dog hookworm. It is dangerous to humans and cats. It also has teeth by which it attaches itself to the intestines of the dog. It changes the site of its attachment about six times a day and the dog loses blood from each detachment, possibly causing iron-deficiency anaemia. Hookworms are easily purged from the dog with many medications. Milbemycin oxime, which also serves as a heartworm preventative in Collies, can be used for this purpose.

In Britain the 'temperate climate' hookworm (*Uncinaria stenocephala*) is rarely found in pet or show dogs, but can occur in hunting packs, racing Greyhounds and sheepdogs because the worms can be prevalent wherever dogs are exercised regularly on grassland.

Did You Know?

Caring for the puppy starts before the puppy is born by keeping the dam healthy and well-nourished. Most puppies have worms, even if they are not evident, so a worming programme is essential. The worms continually shed eggs except during their dormant stage, when they just rest in the tissues of the puppy. During this stage they are not evident during a routine examination.

PHOTO BY C. JAMES WEBB/PHOTOTAKE.

Did You Know?

Average size dogs can pass 1,360,000 roundworm eggs every day.

For example, if there were only 1 million dogs in the world, the world would be saturated with 1,300 metric tonnes of dog faeces.

These faeces would contain 15,000,000,000 roundworm eggs.

7–31% of home gardens and children's play boxes in the U. S. contain roundworm eggs.

Flushing dog's faeces down the toilet is not a safe practice because the usual sewage treatments do not destroy roundworm eggs.

Infected puppies start shedding roundworm eggs at 3 weeks of age. They can be infected by their mother's milk.

The infective stage of the hookworm larva.

The head and rostellum (the round prominence on the scolex) of a tapeworm, which infects dogs and humans.

TAPEWORMS

There are many species of tapeworms. They are carried by fleas! The dog eats the flea and starts the tapeworm cycle. Humans can also be infected with tapeworms, so don't eat fleas! Fleas are so small that your dog could pass them onto your hands, your plate or your food and thus make it possible for you to ingest a flea which is carrying tapeworm eggs.

While tapeworm infection is not life threatening in dogs (smart parasite!), it can be the cause of a very serious liver disease for humans. About 50 percent of the humans infected with *Echinococ-*

PHOTO BY CAROLINA BIOLOGICAL SUPPLY/PHOTOTAKE.

cus multilocularis, a type of tapeworm that causes alveolar hydatis, perish.

HEARTWORMS

Heartworms are thin, extended worms up to 30 cms (12 ins) long which live in a dog's heart and the major blood vessels surrounding it. Dogs may have up to 200 of these worms. The symptoms may be loss of energy, loss of appetite, coughing, the development of a pot belly and anaemia.

Heartworms are transmitted by mosquitoes. The mosquito drinks the blood of an infected dog and takes in larvae with the blood. The larvae, called microfilaria, develop within the body of the mosquito and are passed on to the next dog bitten after the larvae mature. It takes two to three weeks for the larvae to develop to the infective stage within the body of the mosquito. Dogs should be treated at about six weeks of age, then every six months.

Blood testing for heartworms is not necessarily indicative of

Did You Know?

Humans, rats, squirrels, foxes, coyotes, wolves, mixed breeds of dogs and purebred dogs are all susceptible to tapeworm infection. Except in humans, tapeworms are usually not a fatal infection.

Infected individuals can harbour a thousand parasitic worms.

Tapeworms have two sexes—male and female (many other worms have only one sex—male and female in the same worm).

If dogs eat infected rats or mice, they get the tapeworm disease.

One month after attaching to a dog's intestine, the worm starts shedding eggs. These eggs are infective immediately.

Infective eggs can live for a few months without a host animal.

Roundworms, whipworms and tapeworms are just a few of the other commonly known worms that infect dogs.

how seriously your dog is infected. This is a dangerous disease. Although heartworm is a problem for dogs in America, Australia, Asia and Central Europe, dogs in the United Kingdom are not affected by heartworm.

The heartworm, *Dirofilaria immitis*.

PHOTO BY JAMES E HAYDEN, RPB/PHOTOTAKE

Magnified
heartworm
larvae,
*Dirofilaria
immitis.*

PHOTO BY CAROLINA BIOLOGICAL SUPPLY/PHOTOTAKE.

The heart
of a dog infected
with canine
heartworm,
Dirofilaria immitis.

PHOTO BY JAMES E HAYDEN, RPB/PHOTOTAKE.

133

BREED-RELATED HEREDITARY CONDITIONS

HIP DYSPLASIA

This is a congenital problem whereby the acetabulum (hip socket), into which the femoral head (knucklebone) rests, degenerates. It can only be diagnosed by scrutiny of an x-ray by specialists trained to do so. The BVA (British Veterinary Association) manages a joint scheme with The Kennel Club, and on the Continent the universities in the various countries have established, together with the FCI (Fédération Cynologique Internationale), international classifications.

Most breeders x-ray all the dogs they use for breeding and eliminate those dogs with a high hip score from their breeding programme.

PROGRESSIVE RETINAL ATROPHY (PRA)

PRA is a congenital disease of the eye that is causing much concern in canine circles. It is inherited through a recessive gene, i.e., both parents must be carriers of the gene to produce affected offspring. The symptoms rarely manifest themselves until a dog is mature, sometimes even at six or seven years of age, so that the dog or bitch may well have been used for breeding. The disease can only be diagnosed by a specialist with special equipment. In many countries, eye testing is obligatory if

DO YOU KNOW ABOUT HIP DYSPLASIA?

Hip dysplasia is a fairly common condition found in purebred dogs. When a dog has hip dysplasia, its hind leg has an incorrectly formed hip joint. By constant use of the hip joint, it becomes more and more loose, wears abnormally and may become arthritic.

Hip dysplasia can only be confirmed with an x-ray, but certain symptoms may indicate a problem. Your dog may have a hip dysplasia problem if it walks in a peculiar manner, hops instead of smoothly runs, uses his hind legs in unison (to keep the pressure off the weak joint), has trouble getting up from a prone position or always sits with both legs together on one side of its body.

As the dog matures, it may adapt well to life with a bad hip, but in a few years the arthritis develops and many dogs with hip dysplasia become cripples.

Hip dysplasia is considered an inherited disease and can usually be diagnosed when the dog is three to nine months old. Some experts claim that a special diet might help your puppy outgrow the bad hip, but the usual treatments are surgical. The removal of the pectineus muscle, the removal of the round part of the femur, reconstructing the pelvis and replacing the hip with an artificial one are all surgical interventions that are expensive, but they are usually very successful. Follow the advice of your veterinary surgeon.

HIP DYSPLASIA

Compare the two hip joints and you'll understand dysplasia better. Hip dysplasia is a badly worn hip joint caused by inproper fit of the bone into the socket. It is easily the most common hip problem in English Springer Spaniels.

The illustration shows a healthy hip joint on the left and an unhealthy hip joint on the right.

Hip dysplasia can only be positively diagnosed by x-ray. English Springer Spaniels manifest the problem when they are between four and nine months of age, the so-called fast growth period.

English Springer Spaniel

Springers love to swim, but should not be allowed in water that appears polluted. Harmful bacteria, which can cause your dog to become sick, are sometimes found in lakes and ponds.

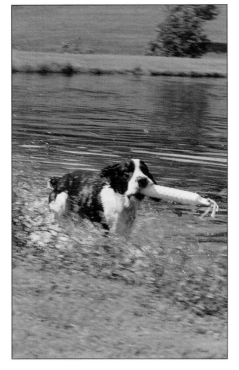

Opposite page: A scanning electron micrograph image of typical dog hairs, enlarged 600 times. These are healthy hairs, evidenced by the cuticles' being neat and uniform. SEM by Dr Dennis Kunkel, University of Hawaii.

one wants to breed and the results of the eye-tests are published in a veterinary dog journal.

CATARACTS

Cataract is a condition whereby the lens of the eyes becomes covered with a milky film and the dog's eyesight is seriously affected. It is often found in older dogs. However, cataract can also be inherited and affect young Springers. Dogs that are being tested for PRA will normally also be tested for cataract. Contrary to PRA, cataracts can occur in one eye only.

RETINAL DYSPLASIA (RD)

RD in its simplest form is seen as a multiple folding of the retina, whilst the most severe form is non-attachment of the retina to the underlying choroid. The effect on sight varies from no apparent effect to total blindness. Testing on RD can be done in the litter, although the test, the same as the tests on PRA and cataracts, has to be repeated annually.

CANINE FUCOSIDOSIS

This disease was first noticed in 1980 in Australia where both English Springers and humans were affected. Affected dogs show loss of weight, increasing wobbliness of gait, odd muscle spasms and increasing difficulty in eating. There is no known cure for the disease but it can be diagnosed easily. The cause is a deficiency of a certain enzyme or chemical that is essential for the breakdown of a sugar (fucose) in body cells. Affected dogs are born without the gene that produces this enzyme. A blood test can determine whether a dog is a carrier for this disease. Responsible breeders have been very careful in their breeding and have brought the problem under control. Affected dogs suffer emaciation, neurological defects and cerebral degeneration within the first two years of life.

S. E. M. BY DR DENNIS KUNKEL, UNIVERSITY OF HAWAII

The term *old* is a qualitative term. For dogs, as well as their masters, old is relative. Certainly we can all distinguish between a puppy English Springer Spaniel and an adult Springer—there are the obvious physical traits, such as size, appearance and facial expressions, and personality traits. Puppies that are nasty are very rare. Puppies and young dogs like to play with children. Children's natural exuberance is a good match for the seemingly endless energy of young dogs. They like to run, jump, chase and retrieve. When dogs grow up and cease their interaction with children, they are often thought of as being too old to play with the kids.

On the other hand, if an English Springer Spaniel is only exposed to people over 60 years of age, its life will normally be less active and it will not seem to be getting old as its activity level slows down.

If people live to be 100 years old, dogs live to be 20 years old. Whilst this is a good rule of thumb, it is very inaccurate. When trying to compare dog years to human years, you cannot make a generalisation about all dogs. You can make the generalisation that 13 years is a good life span for an English Springer Spaniel, which is quite good compared to many other purebred dogs that may only live to eight or nine years of age. Some Springers have been known to live to 20 years. Dogs are generally considered mature within three years, but they can reproduce even earlier. So the first three years of a dog's life are like seven times that of comparable humans. That means a 3-year-old dog is like a 21-year-old human. As the curve of comparison shows, there is no hard and fast rule for comparing dog and human ages. The comparison is made even more difficult, for not all humans age at the same rate...and human females live longer than human males.

Did You Know?

The bottom line is simply that a dog is getting old when YOU think it is getting old because it slows down in its general activities, including walking, running, eating, jumping and retrieving. On the other hand, certain activities increase, such as more sleeping, more barking and more repetition of habits like going to the door without being called when you put your coat on to leave or go outdoors.

WHAT TO LOOK FOR IN SENIORS

Most veterinary surgeons and behaviourists use the seventh year mark as the time to consider a dog a 'senior.' The term 'senior' does not imply that the dog is geriatric and has begun to fail in mind and body. Ageing is essentially a slowing process. Humans readily admit that they feel a difference in their activity level from age 20 to 30, and then from 30 to 40, etc. By treating the seven-year-old dog as a senior, owners are able to implement certain therapeutic and preventive medical strategies with the help of their veterinary surgeons. A senior-care programme should include at least two veterinary visits per year, screening sessions to determine the dog's health status, as well as nutritional counselling. Veterinary surgeons determine the senior dog's health status through a blood smear for a complete blood count, serum chemistry profile with electrolytes, urinalysis, blood pressure check, electrocardiogram, ocular tonometry (pressure on the eyeball), and dental prophylaxis.

Such an extensive programme for senior dogs is well advised before owners start to see the obvious physical signs of ageing, such as slower and inhibited movement, greying, increased sleep/nap periods, and disinterest in play and other activity. This preventative programme promises a longer, healthier life for the ageing dog. Amongst the physical problems common in ageing dogs are the loss of hearing and vision, arthritis, kidney and liver failure, diabetes mellitus, heart disease, and Cushing's disease (an hormonal disease).

In addition to the physical manifestations discussed, there are some behavioural changes and problems related to ageing dogs. Dogs suffering from hearing or vision loss, dental discomfort or arthritis can become aggressive. Likewise the near-deaf and/or blind dog may be startled more easily and react in an unexpectedly aggressive manner. Seniors suffering from senility can become

As your Springer gets older, do not expect that he will maintain the same amount of energy and activity.

139

more impatient and irritable. Housesoiling accidents are associated with loss of mobility, kidney problems, loss of sphincter control as well as plaque accumulation, physiological brain changes, and reactions to medications. Older dogs, just like young puppies, suffer from separation anxiety, which can lead to excessive barking, whining, housesoiling, and destructive behaviour. Seniors may become fearful of everyday sounds, such as vacuum cleaners, heaters, thunder, and passing traffic. Some dogs have difficulty sleeping, due to discomfort, the need for frequent toilet visits, and the like. Owners should avoid spoiling the older dog with too many fatty treats. Obesity is a common problem in older dogs and subtracts years from their lives. Keep the senior dog as trim as possible since excessive weight puts additional stress on the body's vital organs. Some breeders recommend supplementing the diet with foods high in fibre and lower in calories. Adding fresh vegetables and marrow broth to the senior's diet makes a tasty, low-calorie, low-fat supplement. Vets also offer specialty diets for senior dogs that are worth exploring.

Your dog, as he nears his twilight years, needs his owner's patience and good care more than ever. Never punish an older dog for an accident or abnormal behaviour. For all the years of love, protection and companionship that your dog has provided,

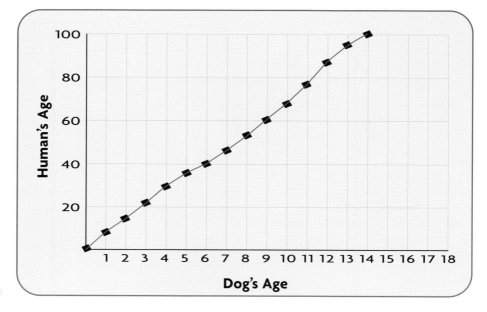

When Your Dog Gets Old...
Signs the Owner Can Look For

IF YOU NOTICE...	IT COULD INDICATE...
Discolouration of teeth and gums, foul breath, loss of appetite	Abcesses, gum disease, mouth lesions
Lumps, bumps, cysts, warts, fatty tumours	Cancers, benign or malignant
Cloudiness of eyes, apparent loss of sight.	Cataracts, lenticular sclerosis, PRA, retinal dysplasia, blindness
Flaky coat, alopaecia (hair loss)	Hormonal problems, hypothyroidism
Obesity, appetite loss, excessive weight gain	Various problems
Household accidents, increased urination	Diabetes, kidney or bladder disease
Increased thirst	Kidney disease, diabetes mellitus
Change in sleeping habits, coughing	Heart disease
Difficulty moving	Arthritis, degenerative joint disease, spondylosis (degenerative spine disease)

If you notice any of these signs, an appointment should be made immediately with a veterinary surgeon for a thorough evaluation.

DID YOU KNOW?

Your senior dog may lose interest in eating, not because he's less hungry but because his senses of smell and taste have diminished. The old chow simply does not smell as good as it once did. Additionally, older dogs use less energy and thereby can sustain themselves on less food.

he deserves special attention and courtesies. The older dog may need to relieve himself at 3 a.m. because he can no longer hold it for eight hours. Older dogs may not be able to remain crated for more than two or three hours. It may be time to give up a sofa or chair to your old friend. Although he may not seem as enthusiastic about your attention and petting, he does appreciate the considerations you offer as he gets older.

Your English Springer Spaniel does not understand why his world is slowing down. Owners must make the transition into the golden years as pleasant and rewarding as possible.

WHAT TO DO WHEN THE TIME COMES

You are never fully prepared to make a rational decision about putting your dog to sleep. It is very obvious that you love your English Springer Spaniel or you would not be reading this book. Putting a loved dog to sleep is extremely difficult. It is a decision that must be made with your veterinary surgeon. You are usually forced to make the decision when one of the life-threatening symptoms listed above becomes serious enough for you to seek medical (veterinary) help.

If the prognosis of the malady indicates the end is near and your beloved pet will only suffer more and experience no enjoyment for the balance of its life, then euthanasia is the right choice.

WHAT IS EUTHANASIA?

Euthanasia derives from the Greek meaning *good death*. In other words, it means the planned, painless killing of a dog suffering from a painful, incurable condition, or who is so aged that it cannot walk, see, eat or control its excretory functions.

Euthanasia is usually accomplished by injection with an overdose of an anaesthesia or barbiturate. Aside from the prick of the needle, the experience is usually painless.

HOW ABOUT YOU?

The decision to euthanize your dog is never easy. The days during which the dog becomes ill and the end occurs can be unusually stressful for you. If this is your first experience with the death of a loved one, you may need the comfort dictated by your religious beliefs. If you are the head of the family and have children, you should have involved them in the decision of putting your English Springer Spaniel to sleep. Usually your dog can be maintained on drugs for a few days in order to give you ample time to make a decision. During this time, talking with members of your family or even people who have lived through this same experience can ease the burden of your inevitable decision.

CDS: COGNITIVE DYSFUNCTION SYNDROME
'Old Dog Syndrome'

There are many ways for you to evaluate old-dog syndrome. Veterinary surgeons have defined CDS (cognitive dysfunction syndrome) as the gradual deterioration of cognitive abilities. These are indicated by changes in the dog's behaviour. When a dog changes its routine response, and maladies have been eliminated as the cause of these behavioural changes, then CDS is the usual diagnosis.

More than half the dogs over 8 years old suffer some form of CDS. The older the dog, the more chance it has of suffering from CDS. In humans, doctors often dismiss the CDS behavioural changes as part of 'winding down.'

There are four major signs of CDS: frequent toilet accidents inside the home, sleeps much more or much less than normal, acts confused, and fails to respond to social stimuli.

SYMPTOMS OF CDS

FREQUENT TOILET ACCIDENTS
- *Urinates in the house.*
- *Defecates in the house.*
- *Doesn't signal that he wants to go out.*

SLEEP PATTERNS
- *Moves much more slowly.*
- *Sleeps more than normal during the day.*
- *Sleeps less during the night.*
- *Walks around listlessly and without a destination goal.*

CONFUSION
- *Goes outside and just stands there.*
- *Appears confused with a faraway look in his eyes.*
- *Hides more often.*
- *Doesn't recognise friends.*
- *Doesn't come when called.*

FAILS TO RESPOND TO SOCIAL STIMULI
- *Comes to people less frequently, whether called or not.*
- *Doesn't tolerate petting for more than a short time.*
- *Doesn't come to the door when you return home from work.*

THE FINAL RESTING PLACE

Dogs can have some of the same privileges as humans. They can occasionally be buried in their entirety in a pet cemetery which is generally expensive, or if they have died at home can buried in your garden in a place suitably marked with some stone or newly planted tree or bush. Alternatively they can be cremated and the ashes returned to you, or some people prefer to leave their dogs at the surgery for the vet to dispose of.

All of these options should be discussed frankly and openly with your veterinary surgeon. Do not be afraid to ask financial questions. Cremations can be individual, but a less expensive option is mass cremation, although of course the ashes can not then be returned. Vets can usually arrange cremation services on your behalf, but you must be aware that in Britain if your dog has died at the surgery the vet legally cannot allow you to take your dog's body home.

GETTING ANOTHER DOG?

The grief of losing your beloved dog will be as lasting as the grief of losing a human friend or relative. You cannot go out and buy another grandfather, but you can go out and buy another English Springer Spaniel. In most cases, if your dog died of old age (if there is such a thing), it had slowed down considerably. Do you want a new Springer puppy to replace it? Or are you better off in finding a more mature Springer, say two to three years of age, which will usually be housetrained and will have an already developed personality. In this case, you can find out if you like each other after a few hours of being together.

The decision is, of course, your own. Do you want another English Springer Spaniel or perhaps a different breed so as to avoid comparison with your beloved friend? Most people usually buy the same breed because they know (and love) the characteristics of that breed. Then, too, they often know people who have the same breed and perhaps they are lucky enough that a breeder they know and respect expects a litter soon. What could be better?

Pet cemeteries offer suitable receptacles for dogs' ashes.

When you purchased your English Springer Spaniel you should have made it clear to the breeder whether you wanted one just as a loveable companion and pet, or if you hoped to be buying an English Springer Spaniel with show prospects. No reputable breeder would have sold you a young puppy saying that it was *definitely* of show quality, for so much can go wrong during the early weeks and months of a puppy's development. If you plan to show, what you will hopefully have acquired is a puppy with 'show potential.'

To the novice, exhibiting an English Springer Spaniel in the show ring may look easy but it usually takes a lot of hard work and devotion to do top winning at a show such as the prestigious Crufts, not to mention a little luck too!

The first concept that the canine novice learns when watching a dog show is that each dog first competes against members of its own breed. Once the judge has selected the best member of each breed, provided that the show is judged on a Group system, that chosen dog will compete with other dogs in its group. Finally the best of each group will com-

pete for Best in Show and Reserve Best in Show.

The second concept that you must understand is that the dogs are not actually compared to one another. The judge compares each dog against the breed standard, which is a written description of the ideal specimen of the breed. Whilst some early breed standards were indeed based on specific dogs that were famous or popular, many dedicated enthusiasts say that a perfect specimen, described in the standard, has never been bred. Thus the 'perfect' dog never walked into a show ring, has never been bred and, to the woe of dog breeders around the globe, does not exist. Breeders attempt to get as close to this ideal as possible, with every litter, but theoretically the 'perfect' dog is so elusive that it is impossible. (And if the 'perfect' dog were born, breeders and judges would never agree that it was indeed 'perfect.')

If you are interested in exploring dog shows, your best bet is to join your local breed club. These clubs often host both Championship and Open shows, and sometimes Match meetings and Special Events, all of which could be of interest, even if you are only an onlooker. Clubs also send out

145

An outdoor dog show in the Netherlands, featuring spaniels of all varieties.

newsletters and some organise training days and seminars in order that people may learn more about their chosen breed. To locate the nearest breed club for you, contact The Kennel Club, the ruling body for the British dog world. The Kennel Club governs not only conformation shows but also working trials, obedience trials, agility trials and field trials. The Kennel Club furnishes the rules and regulations for all these events plus general dog registration and other basic requirements of dog ownership. Its annual show called the Crufts Dogs Show, held in Birmingham, is the largest bench show in England. Every year around 20,000 of the UK's best dogs qualify to participate in this marvellous show which lasts four days.

The Kennel Club governs many different kinds of shows in Great Britain, Australia, South Africa and beyond. At the most competitive and prestigious of these shows, the Championship Shows, a dog can earn Challenge Certificates, and thereby become a Show Champion or a Champion. A dog must earn three Challenge Certificates under three different judges to earn the prefix of 'Sh Ch' or 'Ch.' Note that some breeds, including Gundogs, must also qualify in a field trial in order to gain the title of full champion. Challenge Certificates are awarded to a very small percentage of the dogs competing, especially as dogs which are already Champions compete with others for these coveted CCs. The number of Challenge Certificates awarded in any one year is based upon the total number of dogs in each breed entered for competition. There are three types of Championship Shows: an all-breed General Championship show for all Kennel-Club-recognised breeds; a Group Championship Show, limited to breeds within one of the Groups; and a Breed Show, usually confined to a single breed. The Kennel Club determines which breeds at which Championship Shows will have the opportunity to earn Challenge Certificates (or tickets). Serious exhibitors often will opt not to participate if the tickets are withheld at a particular show. This policy makes earning championships ever more difficult to accomplish.

Open Shows are generally less competitive and are frequently used as 'practice shows' for young dogs. There are hundreds of Open Shows each year that can be invitingly social events and are great first show experiences for the novice. Even if you're considering just watching a show to wet your paws, an Open Show is a great choice.

Whilst Championship and Open Shows are most important for the beginner to understand, there are other types of shows in which the interested dog owner can participate. Training clubs sponsor Matches that can be entered on the day of the show for a nominal fee. In these introductory-level exhibitions, two dogs are pulled out of a hat and 'matched,' the winner of that match goes on to the next round, and eventually only one dog is left undefeated.

Exemption Shows are much more light-hearted affairs with usually only four pedigree classes and several 'fun' classes, all of which can be entered on the day. The proceeds of an Exemption Show must be given to a charity and are sometimes held in conjunction with small agricultural shows. Limited Shows are also available in small numbers, but entry is restricted to members of the club that hosts the show,

although one can usually join the club when making an entry.

Before you actually step into the ring, you would be well advised to sit back and observe the judge's ring procedure. If it is your first time in the ring, do not be over-anxious and run to the front of the line. It is much better to stand back and study how the exhibitor in front of you is performing. The judge asks each handler to 'stand' the dog, hopefully showing the dog off to his best advantage. The judge will observe the dog from a distance and from different angles, approach the dog, check his teeth, overall structure, alertness and muscle tone, as well as consider how well the dog 'conforms' to the standard. Most importantly, the judge will have the exhibitor move the dog around the ring in some pattern that he or she should specify (another advantage to not going first, but always listen since some judges change their directions, and the judge is always right!) Finally the judge will give the dog one last look before moving on to the next exhibitor.

If you are not in the top three at your first show, do not be discouraged. Be patient and consistent and you may eventually find yourself in the winning line-up. Remember that the winners were once in your shoes and have devoted many hours and much money to earn the placement. If you find that your dog is losing every time and never getting a nod, it may be time to consider a different dog sport or just enjoy your English Springer Spaniel as a pet.

WORKING TRIALS

Working trials can be entered by any well-trained dog of any breed, not just Gundogs or Working dogs. Many dogs that earn The Kennel Club Good Citizen Dog award choose to participate in a working trial. There are three stakes at both open and championship levels: Companion Dog (CD), Utility Dog (UD) and Working Dog (WD), Like in conformation shows, dogs compete against a standard and if the dog reaches the qualifying mark, it obtains a certificate.

Divided into groups, each exercise must be achieved 70 percent in order to qualify. If the dog achieves 80 percent in the open level, it receives a Certificate of Merit (COM); in the championship level, it receives a Qualifying Certificate. At the CD stake, dogs must participate in four groups, Control, Stays, Agility and Retrieving, and Nosework. At the next three levels, UD, WD and TD, there are only three groups: Control, Agility and Nosework.

Agility consists of three jumps: a vertical scale up a six-foot wall of planks; a clear jump across a basic three-foot hurdle with a removable top bar; and a long jump of angled planks stretching nine feet.

A Springer is gaited by his handler as the judge evaluates the dog's movement.

To earn the UD and WD dogs must track approximately one-half mile for articles laid from one-half hour to three hours ago. Tracks consist of turns and legs, and fresh ground is used for each participant.

WORKING TESTS

Working tests are frequently used to prepare dogs for field trials, the purpose of which is to heighten the instincts and natural abilities of gundogs. Live game is not used in working tests. Unlike field trials, working tests do not count toward a dog's record at The Kennel Club, though the same judges often oversee working tests. Field trials began in England in 1947

Did You Know?

You can get information about dog shows from kennel clubs and breed clubs:

Fédération Cynologique Internationale
14, rue Leopold II, B-6530 Thuin, Belgium
www.fci.be

The Kennel Club
1-5 Clarges St., Piccadilly, London W1Y 8AB, UK
www.the-kennel-club.org.uk

American Kennel Club
5580 Centerview Dr., Raleigh, NC 27606-3390, USA
www.akc.org

Canadian Kennel Club
89 Skyway Ave., Suite 100, Etobicoke, Ontario M9W 6R4 Canada
www.ckc.ca

and are only moderately popular amongst dog folk. Whilst breeders of Working and Gundog breeds concern themselves with the field abilities of their dogs, there is considerably less interest in field trials than dog shows.

SPANIEL TRIALS

A spaniel trial is an event with two judges, whereby the dogs work in pairs, one under each judge. After they have finished, they change places so that every dog has worked under both judges.

The spaniel must hunt the ground thoroughly, approximately 15 metres to each side of the handler, so that the game he flushes is within shooting range. He must investigate all cover and if he misses game he will be marked down.

He must sit or drop when he flushes game, as well as to allow a shot. He must retrieve the game on command. Chasing the game and having a hard mouth disqualifies as does 'giving tongue,' which is whining, barking, etc. In some European countries, giving tongue is a requirement for a spaniel.

FIELD TRIALS

Should your pupil really be talented, you can go on from working tests to train him for field trials. It will take a lot of your time, patience and dedication but the rewards are well worth it.

Show Ring Etiquette

Just like with anything else, there is a certain etiquette to the show ring that can only be learned through experience. Showing your dog can be quite intimidating to you as a novice when it seems as if everyone else knows what they are doing. You can familiarise yourself with ring procedure beforehand by taking a class to prepare you and your dog for conformation showing or by talking with an experienced handler. When you are in the ring, listen and pay attention to the judge and follow his/her directions. Remember, even the most skilled handlers had to start somewhere. Keep it up and you too will become a proficient handler before too long!

At a field trial, your dog must be under control at all times, work his ground with speed and style and is expected to retrieve from water.

A dog becomes a Field Trial Champion when he has won two Open or All Ages Stakes or when he wins the Spaniel Championship.

SNIFFER DOGS

A new career has been discovered for Springer Spaniels as sniffer dogs. Sniffer dogs are used to find drugs, explosives and recently also cigarettes that are hidden in cars, luggage and freight.

Several hundreds of dogs are being trained each year. For a greater part, the training runs on

parallel lines with the gundog training, i.e., as far as the dogs discovering the quarry. The dogs are being trained with dummies that contain a quantity of the target substance.

It seems that the Springers have taken over this job from the retrievers, Springers having better scenting powers and being able to work fully concentrated for longer periods.

Springer Spaniels have recently found work as 'sniffer' dogs, used for drug and explosive detection. It's easy to see why they are perfect for this difficult and important job.

TRACKING

In tracking trials dogs are being tested on their ability to trail and find game. The dogs are tested individually and the trail must be followed at a sensible pace, neither too fast nor too slow.

This is what it's all about! A Springer strikes a winning pose in the show ring.

Tracking has become very popular; especially in Norway, where it is considered to be an excellent way of finding wounded deer and elk, and in the U.S., where it has become a popular competition sport.

AGILITY TRIALS

Agility trials began in the United Kingdom in 1977 and have since spread around the world, especially to the U.S., where it enjoys strong popularity. The handler directs his dog over an obstacle course that includes jumps (such as those used in the working trials), as well as tyres, the dog walk, weave poles, pipe tunnels, collapsed tunnels, etc. The Kennel Club requires that dogs not be trained for agility until they are 12 months old. This dog sport intends to be great fun for dog and owner and interested owners should join a training club that has obstacles and experienced agility handlers who can introduce you and your dog to the 'ropes' (and tyres, tunnels and so on).

Different obstacles at an agility trial: (top) weave poles, (middle) see-saw and (bottom) bar jump.

FÉDÉRATION CYNOLOGIQUE INTERNATIONALE

Established in 1911, the Fédération Cynologique Internationale (FCI) represents the 'world kennel club.' This international body brings uniformity to the breeding, judging and showing of purebred dogs.

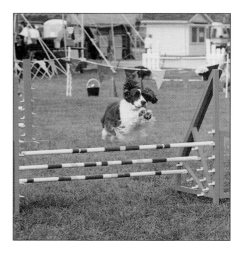

Did You Know?

There are 329 breeds recognised by the FCI, and each breed is considered to be 'owned' by a specific country. Each breed standard is a cooperative effort between the breed's country and the FCI's Standards and Scientific Commissions. Judges use these official breed standards at shows held in FCI member countries. One of the functions of the FCI is to update and translate the breed standards into French, English, Spanish and German.

What a wonderful reward when your English Springer Spaniel is both a beloved pet and a winner in the show ring!

A Dutch champion English Springer Spaniel poses with his handler and the judge.

The main goal of this book is to help you train and care for your dog as a pet and companion. The choice to show or compete with your Springer is completely yours—good luck with your endeavours!

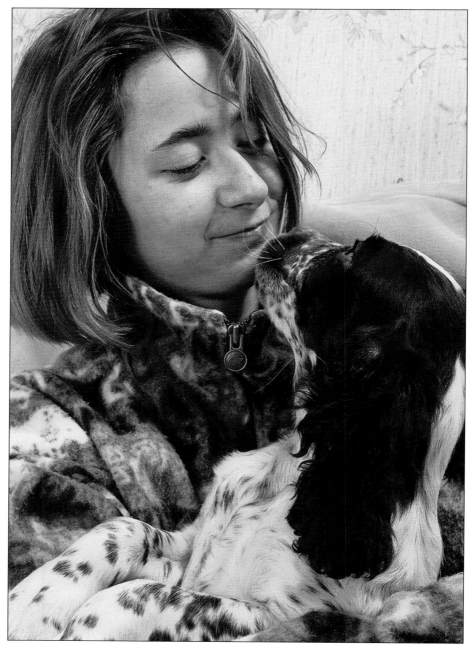

Did You Know?

In Britain, here can be as many as 18 classes per sex for your breed. Check the show schedule carefully to make sure that you have entered your dog in the appropriate class. Among the classes offered can be: Beginners; Minor Puppy (ages 6 to 9 months); Puppy (ages 6 to 12 months); Junior (ages 6 to 18 months); Beginners (handler or dog never won first place) as well as the following, each of which is defined in the schedule: Maiden; Novice; Tyro; Debutant; Undergraduate; Graduate; Postgraduate; Minor Limit; Mid Limit; Limit; Open; Veteran; Stud Dog; Brood Bitch; Progeny; Brace and Team.

Although the FCI originally included only four European nations: France, Holland, Austria and Belgium (which remains its headquarters), the organisation today embraces nations on six continents and recognises well over 300 breeds of purebred dog. There are three titles attainable through the FCI: the International Champion, which is the most prestigious; the International Beauty Champion, which is based on aptitude certificates in different countries; and the International Trial Champion, which is based on achievement in obedience trials in different countries. Quarantine laws in England and Australia prohibit most of their exhibitors from entering FCI shows. The rest of the European nations do participate in these impressive canine spectacles, the largest of which is the World Dog Show, hosted in a different country each year. FCI sponsors both national and international shows. The hosting country determines the judging system and breed standards are always based on the breed's country of origin.

Did You Know?

The FCI *does not* issue pedigrees. The FCI members and contract partners are responsible for issuing pedigrees and training judges in their own countries. The FCI does maintain a list of judges and makes sure that they are recognised throughout the FCI member countries.

The FCI also *does not* act as a breeder referral; breeder information is available from FCI-recognised national canine societies in each of the FCI's member countries.

INDEX
*Page numbers in **boldface** indicate illustrations.*

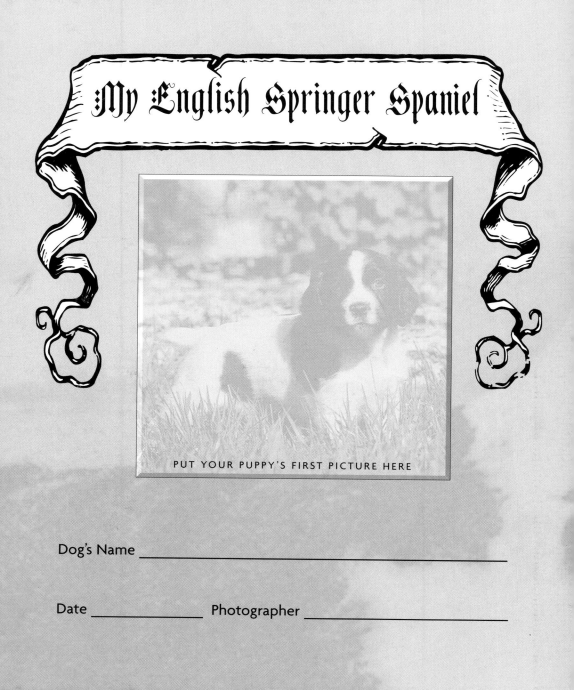

My English Springer Spaniel

PUT YOUR PUPPY'S FIRST PICTURE HERE

Dog's Name _____

Date _____ Photographer _____